Arnoldo Van Westerhout incise

FILIPPO BONANNI

Antique Musical Instruments and Their Players

152 Plates from Bonanni's
18th Century "Gabinetto Armonico"

With
a new Introduction
and Captions by

FRANK Ll. HARRISON
and JOAN RIMMER

DOVER PUBLICATIONS, INC.

NEW YORK

Published in Canada by General Publishing Company, Ltd., 30 Lesmill Road, Don Mills, Toronto, Ontario.

Published in the United Kingdom by Constable and Company, Ltd., 10 Orange Street, London WC 2.

This Dover edition, first published in 1964, contains all the engravings from the revised and enlarged *Gabinetto Armonico* as published in Rome in 1723. The new introduction and explanatory text were written specially for this edition by Frank Ll. Harrison and Joan Rimmer. The illustration reproduced as a frontispiece to this edition represents King David, to whom the work was dedicated.

International Standard Book Number: 0-486-21179-7
Library of Congress Catalog Card Number: 63-19491

Manufactured in the United States of America
Dover Publications, Inc.
180 Varick Street
New York, N.Y. 10014

Introduction

Filippo Bonanni was born in Rome in 1658, became a Jesuit, and in 1698 was appointed curator of the collection of antiquities formed by the celebrated Athanasius Kircher and preserved in the Jesuit College. One of Kircher's many writings was a compendious but unreliable work on music called *Musurgia Universalis* (two volumes, 1650). It may have been from this work, which had a number of engravings of musical instruments, that Bonanni got the idea for his *Gabinetto Armonico*. This was the last of a series of illustrated publications by Bonanni which had included works on natural history, architectural history and the history of religious, military and chivalric orders and their dress.

The *Gabinetto Armonico*, first printed in 1716 and revised and expanded in 1723, was reprinted in Paris in 1776 with a French translation alongside a reduced version of the original commentary. It has been deprecated by many historians of instruments—somewhat unjustly, one feels, after studying it closely. Even though inexact in detail at times, it is more truly comprehensive than any book on musical instruments until the work of Curt Sachs.* Unlike earlier books on the subject it is entirely non-professional in its approach. Neither didactic, nor scientific in the seventeenth-century sense, it has a humanistic attitude and sociological awareness which anticipate some of the most progressive features of organology today.

The scope of the *Gabinetto Armonico* reveals its author's open-mindedness in accepting material from all levels of European society and from many cultures outside it. Bonanni gives art and folk instruments of Europe, naturally with an Italian emphasis, many little-known instruments used in the Eastern Christian churches, and a remarkably

---

* Sachs's *Real-Lexikon der Musikinstrumente*, with additions and revisions by Sachs, will be republished by Dover Publications in 1964.

wide coverage of extra-European material. His sources are corre-
spondingly varied. They include scholarly works on liturgy and cam-
panology and accounts of foreign journeys by travellers and diplomats.
Besides Kircher, Bonanni's most important written musical source
is Marin Mersenne, the French philosopher and mathematician whose
Harmonie Universelle of 1636–67 has a detailed section on instruments.
He does not seem to have been familiar with the instrumental section,
published in 1619, of the *Syntagma Musicum* of Michael Praetorius. Four
of Bonanni's non-European instruments which also appear in the
Syntagma were probably taken from a common source.

For this reprint of the plates from the *Gabinetto Armonico* no attempt
has been made to translate the original commentary, with its weight of
classical allusion and quotation. Instead, the authors have tried to
accompany the splendid engravings of Arnold van Westerhout with
brief but informative captions.

Oxford, 1963   F. Ll. H.

                                                   J. R.

List of Plates

I

The *HEBREW TRUMPET*, like the Egyptian trumpet of which some examples and many pictures survive, was a conical tube of metal, bell-ended, and, according to Flavius Josephus, "a little less than a cubit long." Trumpets were used in the elaborate musical ritual of the Temple, but their function was to produce a loud and brilliant blare rather than a controlled musical sound in the modern sense.

I   *Tromba antica Ebrea*

2

The *ROMAN TRUMPET*, made of bronze, was longer than the Hebrew trumpet but not essentially different. Its use seems to have been entirely military and gladiatorial, and its sound raucous.

II *Tromba Romana antica*

3

This plate, taken by Bonanni's engraver from a figure on the Capitol, does not show a trumpet. It shows incorrectly the *DOUBLE AULOS*, which has been the most misrepresented and mistranslated of all the instruments of antiquity. Its pipes were cylindrical in bore and were sounded by very large double reeds. As the acoustic behaviour of a reed instrument is determined by its bore and not by its reed, the aulos was basically of the clarinet family, with a low pitch for its size. Modern experiments with casts of ancient double pipes show that the sound was rich and full, and certainly clarinettish in quality, not screaming and oboe-like as has often been asserted. Pipes of this type were the high art wind instruments of the Sumerian, Egyptian, Greek and Roman civilisations. They became obsolete—except for folk survivals—with the development in the early centuries of the Christian era of the more extended and mobile conical reed pipe, the predecessor of the modern oboe.

III   *Tromba antica espressa nel Campidoglio*

4

This is the *TRUMPET* of the early eighteenth century, a seven-foot length of brass or silver looped into a convenient shape. In Bonanni's time, besides military trumpeters who played fanfares and flourishes of a fairly simple nature, there were, especially in Germany, specialist players of the instrument's highest, or *clarino* register. This exclusive and virtuoso style disappeared in the second half of the eighteenth century, leaving a period of simple middle register trumpet playing until the invention of valves gave the instrument a large and foolproof compass.

IV   *Tromba doppia*

ʃ

The *TROMBONE*, in principle a trumpet with a movable U-shaped tube which fits into the main body of the instrument, was established in something fairly like its present form by 1500. Under its original name, sackbut, it played the bass or tenor part in the shawm consorts used for ceremonial and dance music in the sixteenth century, and it was made in several sizes for German wind bands. The plate shows a bass trombone.

49

V   *Tromba Spezzata*

6

By the fifteenth century a *SLIDE TRUMPET* was in use, with a long tube at the mouthpiece end which fitted telescopically into the body of the instrument. By moving the instrument in and out the player could obtain a larger range of contiguous notes than was possible on the ordinary trumpet. It cannot, however, have been a very satisfactory instrument, though it survived in Germany up to Bonanni's time and was used by Bach, under the name *tromba da tirarsi*, in several cantatas.

VI   *Altra Tromba Spezzata*

7

The Roman *CORNU* was a G-shaped conical tube of bronze, used on military and solemn civil occasions. Horace described its sound as a menacing murmur. Bonanni's engraver has given it the zoomorphic head which is also characteristic of the Celtic *carnyx*.

VII   *Tromba curua*

8

This *CORNU* has the wooden crossbar, or carrying crutch, which supported the eleven-foot-long tube on the player's shoulder.

53

VIII   *Altra Tromba piegata antica*

9

The *PERSIAN TRUMPET*, as Bonanni says, "is longer than the player." Trumpets of this kind, used with shawms and drums, provided the Saracen military music which so astounded the Crusaders when they first heard it. The ancient style of playing, in intermittent one-note blasts an octave below the tune-playing shawms, can still be heard in some Persian bands.

IX   *Tromba Perſiana*

There have been many outside influences on the instruments of India, and this *INDIAN TRUMPET*, whose telescopic sections are suggested in the plate though the usual bulbous decorations are not shown, is little different from certain Chinese trumpets. Bonanni points out that the playing position is incorrectly shown—the instrument should be pointing upwards.

X   *Tromba del Madurè*

II

The Roman *LITUUS* is thought to be of Etruscan origin. Although made of one tube expanding to form an upturned flare at the end, it retained the shape of its primitive predecessor, a cane tube whose sound was amplified by the addition of an animal horn. A bronze lituus is preserved in the Vatican Library and hooked bronze instruments of similar type are in the National Museum of Ireland.

54

XI   *Lituo degli Antichi*

12

Bonanni describes this small *HUNTING HORN*, of the kind used by shepherds to call their flocks, as the instrument with which Romulus called together the people of Rome. When made in metal it still retained the shape of its cow horn ancestor.

56

XII   *Corno per la Caccia*   e XIII

13 & 14

This is intended to be a Turkish instrument like the Indian trumpet in appearance, and very difficult to play because it "needs a great quantity of air to make it sound."

15

This type of *CHINESE TRUMPET* consists of a slender tube inserted in a large cylinder of iron, copper or copper-covered wood.

XV   *Tromba Cinese*

16

Bonanni describes the sound of this small coiled *BUGLE HORN*, used by couriers and huntsmen, as being much clearer than that of the old animal horn.

XVI   *Altro corno per la Caccia*

17

The *FRENCH HORN* of the early eighteenth century was restricted to the hunting field in France, but in Germany and Bohemia it was already being admitted to indoor use in theatre and ensemble music. The simple form shown in this plate survives today in the French *trompe de chasse* used in the hunt and by Alpine regiments.

XVII · *Corno Raddoppiato*

18

The *CONCH SHELL TRUMPET* is used by many primitive peoples, in some cases as a voice amplifier or distorter, in others as a musical sound producer. It generally has a ritual or magical significance, as in India, where it is connected with the god Vishnu. In Europe it is put to humbler and more practical use—the fish sellers of Majorca, for example, announce their wares by blowing a conch. Bonanni gives the Greek legend of the Triton who conquered giants with the terrifying sound of the shell trumpet.

XVIII   *Bucina Marina*

19

This picture of a RECORDER shows the large-bored type which was obsolete in Bonanni's time. It had been superseded in the previous century by the narrower recorders designed by the Hotteterres, who were instrument makers to Louis XIV. The Baroque recorder, with its arch and somewhat innocent sound, vanished from art music in the mid-eighteenth century. Fipple whistles, of which the recorder is a late example, have the longest attested history of all musical instruments. Excavations of the earliest habitation sites of *Homo sapiens* in Europe have yielded hundreds of specimens, made in bird or animal bone, with two or three fingerholes. Simple but robust-toned instruments of this family maintain a vigorous existence as folk instruments in many parts of the world.

Flauto

20

Another inaccurate representation of the DOUBLE AULOS (Latin *tibia*) already shown in Plate 3. Similar incorrect illustrations occur in many books on instruments, those of Praetorius and Mersenne included, and confusion is perpetuated by the exhibition in museums of replicas of these nonsense illustrations. The most fascinating feature of double pipes is the way in which the pipes "reinforce" each other. The tone of each pipe alone is not strong, but together, whether both are melody pipes or one is a drone, they become rich in quality and hypnotic in effect.

XX   *Flauto doppio.*

21

The *TRANSVERSE FLUTE* of Bonanni's time was still that devised by the wind instrument makers of Louis XIV in the previous century. It was gently conical in the opposite direction from that shown in the plate; that is, it was larger at the blowing end and narrower at the foot joint, which carried one key. The older cylindrical flute which is, in fact, what Bonanni describes in his text, was still used in German flute and drum bands. Theobald Boehm, the creator of the modern flute, reintroduced the cylindrical bore in the nineteenth century.

XXI · *Flauto Trauersier*

22

PANPIPES, consisting of graduated tubes of cane, wood, pottery or metal, are of great antiquity and are played over a large part of Europe, Asia and South America. Associated by the Greeks with the goat-footed god Pan, they were rustic instruments throughout the Middle Ages. King David as a shepherd boy is shown with panpipes in some tenth-century manuscripts, and Pyrenean shepherds play them to this day. In Roumania, large wooden panpipes are one of the most important instruments in popular music. Dance tunes and bird-imitating solos are played on them with astonishing agility and brilliance, and their bright, glassy sound is inimitable.

XXII   *Cùfoli Pastorali*

This depiction of the *OBOE* is inaccurate. The oboe of the eighteenth century was the slender, three-jointed, two- or three-keyed instrument created in the mid-seventeenth century by court musicians of Louis XIV. The finger holes and keys are not shown here, while the reed is the large fan-shaped type proper to the old shawm, not the broad reed of the baroque oboe. Bonanni's text goes on to describe the newly invented clarinet (this is the earliest known description) and the small two-keyed chalumeau, though he gives no illustrations of them.

Oboe

24

The text describes the *BASSOON*, which was also a product of the inventive wind instrument makers of Louis XIV, but the illustration, taken from Kircher, is of the old "fagot," a bass of the double reed family which was superseded by the true oboes and bassoons. Confusion arose, and still arises, from the retention of names of older instruments for new ones.

Fagotto

25

Here again the description is of the *TENOR OBOE*, built a fifth lower than the oboe and used in wind bands from the mid-seventeenth century onwards, while the illustration, from Kircher, is of a tenor shawm.

Mezzo Fagotto

26

The *SERPENT*, a conical wooden tube coiled into the serpentine shape from which it took its name, combined the sound-producing method of a brass instrument (that is, from a cup-shaped mouthpiece) with the pitch-changing method of a woodwind instrument (finger-holes on the body of the tube). Invented about 1600 to accompany singing in church, it was later used in military bands. In the mid-nineteenth century the ophicleide and then the tuba took its place, though it lingered for some time in English church bands.

Serpentone

27

These *RUSTIC PIPES* made of oaten straws or of hollowed out stems of fig, laurel or elder, with a vibrating "tongue" cut from the body of the tube itself, are the simplest and most ancient forms of reed instrument. Single pipes of this kind are used as practice instruments by Cretan bagpipers, and Roumanian peasants play elaborate two-part music on double oaten pipes.

Zampogne

Bonanni describes several *BIRD WHISTLES* used as decoys by bird catchers. The cane whistle shown here is, he says, "a modern invention."

XXVIII. *Inſtromento di Canna*

29

This plate shows a bird catcher with a *QUAIL WHISTLE*, made of horsehair inside a small skin bag. When it is squeezed in the hand it emits a quail-like sound.

XXIX

Quagliere

29

Another *BIRD WHISTLE.*

XXIX   *Fischi diversi*

The splendid Italian folk bagpipe called *ZAMPOGNA* is incompletely depicted here. The two chanters are shown but not the two drones, which should emerge from the same stock. Italian pipers of today have been known to use the inner tube of a tyre as a bag, instead of the time-honoured sheepskin. The zampogna is sometimes played by itself, sometimes with a small shawm (see Plate 39).

Piua o Ciaramella

31

The plate shows an impossible bagpipe with neither blowpipe nor bellows to inflate the bag. The text refers to the *SOURDELINE*, or Italian musette, an elaborate bellows-blown chamber bagpipe invented early in the seventeenth century. It had two partly keyed chanters and two completely keyed drones, and so was capable of playing four-part music. This, not the contemporary French chamber bagpipe known as the musette, was the instrument played by Michele Todini (see Plate 33). The sourdeline anticipated many of the characteristic features of the Irish Union Pipes.

XXXI   *Musetta*

32

Because it puts many varieties of sound under the control of one player, the *ORGAN* has long been considered the greatest of musical instruments. The hydraulic organ of the Greeks and Romans elicited admiration for its resources, as in a poem by Claudian in the late fourth century: "Let there be also one who by his light touch manages the unnumbered tongues of the field of brazen tubes, can with nimble fingers cause a mighty sound, and can rouse to song the waters stirred to their depths by the massive lever." The chamber (or "positive") organ of the kind shown here had only wood and open metal pipes, and was noted for sweetness and clarity rather than power. It was widely played in the seventeenth and eighteenth centuries, being made for domestic use both as a solo and an accompanying instrument.

Organo

33

This "organ" was actually a *HARPSICHORD AND THREE SPINETS* playable separately or in any combination from one keyboard. It was made by Michele Todini (fl. *c.* 1650–*c.* 1681), instrument maker and player of the musette (see Plate 31), and was later acquired by Signor Verospi and installed in his palace in Rome, where it was seen but not heard by Dr. Charles Burney, musical historian and father of Fanny, the novelist. Todini devised instruments with complicated mechanisms which he described in his *Dichiaratione della Galleria armonica* (Rome, 1676).

XXXIII *Prospetto della Camera detta Galleria*
in cui sono molti Strumenti sonori, fab.

nica nel Palazzo delli Signori Verospi in Roma
on prodigioso artifizio dà Michele Todino

34

The smallest type of organ, the portative, which was held and blown by the player, is familiar from medieval and Renaissance paintings. The subject of this engraving, however, is a mendicant organ grinder and his *BARREL ORGAN*. The crank handle acted on a cylinder with projections, and also worked a bellows to supply wind for the pipes. A miniature mechanical organ like this could play melody and bass, and had a selection of four or five tunes.

Organo Portatile

35

This imaginary *VOICE AMPLIFIER* is taken directly from Kircher, who suggested that a large elliptical tube would considerably magnify the sound of the voice.

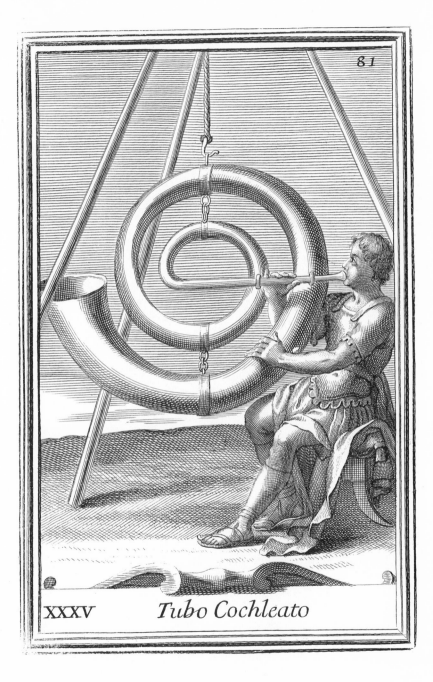

Tubo Cochleato

36

This has no connection with the musical instrument known as the tromba marina (see Plate 62). It is meant to be a *MEGAPHONE* used at sea for the transmission of orders and messages.

Tromba Marina

37

The "*HORN OF ALEXANDER THE GREAT*" is also taken from Kircher, who said that he took it from a manuscript in the Vatican Library. It is not unlike an equally absurd instrument entitled "chorus," which is shown by both Virdung and Praetorius.

XXXVII   *Tubo di Alesandro Magno*

38

This *BUZZER* is made of a length of split cane which, presumably, the player buzzes as children do with a grass blade stretched between their thumbs. Bonanni also describes another in which a small area is cut from a whole cane tube, leaving only a vibrating membrane.

XXXVIII   *Trombetta di Canna*

39

This small Italian *SHAWM*, commonly known as *ciaramella*, is always accompanied by a zampogna, and together they produce a simple but rich polyphony. The lively Christmas tunes of the Italian shepherd bagpipers were the origin of the eighteenth-century pastorales, of which those in Handel's *Messiah*, Bach's *Christmas Oratorio* and Corelli's *Christmas Concerto* are the most familiar. Modern performances of these works, however, rarely give any hint of this robust ancestry.

Ciufolo del Villano

40

A *MARROW TRUMPET*, made from a scooped out marrow (squash) into which is inserted a single-reed tube (see Plate 27). The peasants of Gaeta use it as a hunting and festival instrument.

XL   *Tromba di Zucca*

41

An earthenware *WATER JAR* into which the voice is pitched at the pouring spout, while the hand covers and uncovers the filling aperture to give a change of quality. The jar acts as a resonator to the sound already produced by the voice. This humble instrument, according to Bonanni, "makes an agreeable and stimulating accompaniment to peasant songs and dances."

XLI   *Brocca di Terra*

42

The *COMB AND PAPER*, a universal children's noise maker.

Pettine

43

For three centuries the *HARPSICHORD*, essentially a large mechanised psaltery (see Plate 63), was the most generally useful of the keyboard instruments. It had one, two or, very rarely, three keyboards, and its tonal resources were mechanically contrived, being achieved by the action of various plectra on different groups of strings. Its fixed levels of dynamics were unsuited to the aesthetics of late eighteenth-century music, and it went out of use. The twentieth century's concern with authentic sonorities has brought about its present revival. This and the following illustration give incomplete details of keyboard and mechanism, but are correct in general shape.

Cembalo

44

The small harpsichord with strings disposed vertically, usually called *CLAVICYTHERIUM*, had the advantages, says Bonanni, of needing less space and of being more ornamental as furniture than the large wing-shaped harpsichord. An example in the Metropolitan Museum in New York has folding doors with paintings.

Cembalo Verticale

45

SPINET, a less precise term than harpsichord, was applied to the smaller domestic instruments of the harpsichord type. These varied somewhat in external shape but the strings were always placed at an angle to the keyboard, not following the same direction as in the harpsichord. In England, "virginal" was the usual name for the smaller instruments until the late seventeenth century, while "spinet" was used after that time for the asymmetrically shaped instrument—here simplified into a triangle—which became standard in the eighteenth century. Spinets with two manuals are extremely rare.

XLV *Spinetta*

46

The instrument in this picture is a *LUTE*, not a theorbo. Introduced into Europe in the thirteenth century from Arabian musical culture, the lute had a pear-shaped back, a right-angled peg-box, and four strings or pairs of strings. It was played with a quill or plectrum. The medieval lute was a bright-toned and rather noisy instrument, like the Roumanian popular lute of today. Its character was accurately suggested by Chaucer's references to the lute as an instrument used in taverns. By the sixteenth century it had changed to a rather delicate sounding instrument with a single top string and five double strings, plucked by the fingers. In the hands of a virtuoso player and singer like John Dowland,

> whose heavenly touch
> Upon the lute doth ravish human sense,

the Renaissance lute was both a resourceful solo instrument, capable of playing complex part-music, and an ideal means of intimate self-accompaniment. The theorbo was a larger form of lute devised in the sixteenth century. It had unstopped bass strings carried off the finger-board from a second peg-box, and normally had single strings through-out. Its development reflects the increasing importance of the bass part. It was almost exclusively an accompanying instrument for a soloist or group.

XLVI *Tiorba*

47

The *ARCHLUTE* was still larger than the theorbo and, like it, had bass strings lying off the fingerboard, as shown in the engraving. It could play both bass notes and chordal accompaniment, and was much used for this purpose in solo and chamber music in the seventeenth century. The Italians called the largest size *chitarrone*, the termination *-one* meaning large, as in *violone*. This name is to be distinguished from that of the *chitarrino* (see Plate 60), the termination *-ino* meaning small, as in *violino*.

XLVII *Arcileuto*

48

The cittern was a popular instrument from the sixteenth to the eighteenth century. Its four or five double strings were of metal and could be played by the fingers or with a plectrum. Its music did not go much beyond a cheerful strumming, and its tuning was not unlike that of the banjo today, so that simple chord changes lay easily under the hand. The body had a flat back and pear-shaped outline. Bonanni shows here a *LARGE CITTERN* with ten pairs of strings, a kind which Mersenne says was made by the Italians.

XLVIII   *Cetera*

These are classical Greek *LYRES*, real and imaginary, and a *CITHARA*. All but one are copied from Mersenne. The lyre, correctly shown in the middle row left, had a body of tortoise-shell or wood covered with skin, and arms of animal horn or wood. Its strings were fixed to the crossbar with greasy rolls of leather, which also gave a means of tuning. Lyres of this kind are still made in parts of Africa. Middle row right is a developed cithara with carved sound-box, and a plectrum beside it. It was tuned by adjusting the sticks seen in the engraving. Top row right is the conventional symbolic form of the lyre (see also Plate 52); the other three items are imaginary.

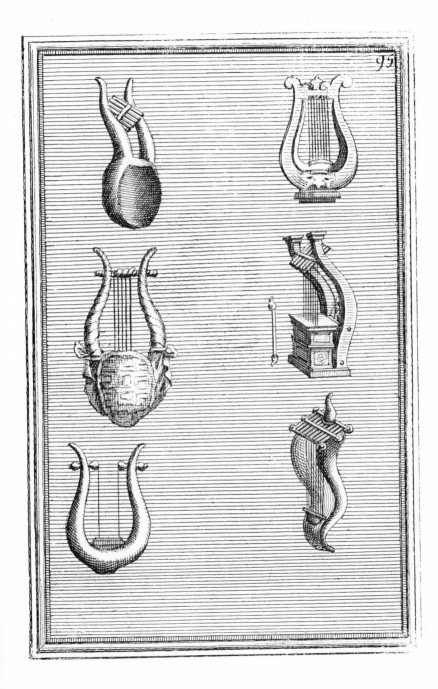

49

Bonanni used the term *pandura*, a late form of a very general ancient term for plucked string instruments (Greek *pandoûra*, Arabic *tanbūr*) for the normal *CITTERN* (see Plate 48). Its contemporary survival is the Portuguese *guitarra* (in Portugal the Spanish guitar is called *viola*).

Pandura

50

Bass instruments of the cittern type included the *BANDORA* (pandora), which Bonanni, following Kircher, here calls "German cittern." These instruments, which were much used in Germany for accompanying during the seventeenth century, did not survive into the eighteenth.

97

L   *Cetera Tedesca*

51

In the seventeenth century the decline of the lute through over-sophistication involved a corresponding rise in the fortunes of the *SPANISH GUITAR*. Five double strings had become standard by the time the fashion for the instrument spread to Italy, France and England. It became a favourite of the aristocratic amateur, as we can see in the paintings of Watteau. The engraving suggests the strongly rhythmic beating across the strings, as used in flamenco, but the guitar was also suited to the playing of courtly dances in an elegant style.

LI   *Chitarra Spagnola*

ʃ 2

The conventional representation of the poet's *LYRE OF APOLLO*, which could have four strings symbolising the elements or seven symbolising the planets.

LII   *Lira di Apollo*

53

Names of instruments of this type have always been loosely applied in
Italy. The mandola (mandora), of which the mandoline is a descendant,
was properly a small lute with four wire strings. The instrument
depicted here is a *SMALL GUITAR*.

Mandola

54

A small *ITALIAN GUITAR* with four or six strings, still played in southern Italy, Spain and Latin America.

LIV   *Chitarrino diuerſo*

♪♪

The *LONG LUTE* used in Arabian, Persian, Indian and Turkish music keeps the ancient Babylonian and Egyptian form, having a small body and long neck. This is still a popular instrument in parts of the Balkans as well as the Orient. An instrument of this type, known as *colascione*, was played in Italy in the sixteenth and seventeenth centuries. Bonanni rightly says that it had two or three strings, although his picture shows five.

Calascione Turchesco

56

In Italian the generic term for all bowed stringed instruments, except the rebec (see Plate 59), was *viola*. In the sixteenth century the two main branches of bowed instruments were known as *viole da gamba* (i.e., played at the leg) and *viole da braccio* (i.e., played on the arm). The former were fretted and flat-backed, and had sloping shoulders and C-shaped sound-holes. The latter developed into our violin family, and the instrument shown here is the bass of that family, then as now called *VIOLONCELLO*.

Viola

57

Here is shown the *DOUBLE-BASS VIOL*, the largest instrument of the gamba family. Bonanni describes it correctly as having six strings, though the engraving shows six pegs but only four strings. The fretted fingerboard characteristic of the viols is clearly shown. This size of viol, and the normal bass commonly known as *viola da gamba*, were the only viols to survive into the eighteenth century.

LVII   *Violone*

58

The name Accordo is a howler. Bonanni took this and the two preceding pictures from a plate in Kircher, which also showed the tunings of the instruments. These were marked Accordo, which Bonanni took to be the name of this instrument. Actually it is a *LIRONE*, a bass instrument modelled on the sixteenth-century *lira da braccio*. This latter had kept the medieval feature of drone strings, and had a body similar in shape to that of the violin. The lirone had twelve strings and two drones (not shown in the engraving, though the pegs are there). This short-lived instrument was especially invented for playing chordal accompaniments. According to Mersenne it was "very languishing and suitable for exciting devotion and causing the spirit to commune with itself; it is used to accompany the voice and recitatives."

LVIII   *Accordo*

59

This instrument is a *KIT*, or dancing master's fiddle, a descendant of the medieval rebec which had come up in the social scale. Like the rebec it had a boat-shaped body, i.e., one without indentations. It is rather too large in the engraving.

102

LIX   *Sordino*

This *chitarrone* is obviously not the bass lute (see Plate 47). The text describes a *LARGE GUITAR*, like those still used in Spain and Latin America. As the engraving intimates, it is a rustic instrument.

LX   *Chitarrone*

61

A *MONOCHORD* ("one-string") existed in classical Greek times, and was used to demonstrate the numerical proportions of the notes of the scale. The Middle Ages revived it, also for teaching purposes. It had a single string between two bridges placed on a sound-box, with a third moveable bridge to show the points of division. Concurrently with this teaching instrument, there existed in the later Middle Ages a performing instrument known as the tromba marina, to which, as Mersenne later pointed out, the term monochord might be applied. This, as seen for example in the Memling altarpiece in Antwerp and in our engraving, was a bowed instrument with two strings. The longer string was touched lightly with a finger or thumb at a point of exact division, so producing harmonics (the sounds of the overtone series). This string passed over a rattling bridge, one leg of which was shorter than the other, so that it vibrated against a metal (or ivory) plate on the body of the instrument. It was bowed above the point of fingering (not below, as shown in the plate), and the shorter string was presumably sounded as a drone.

Monocordo

62

The term *TROMBA MARINA* was also applied to the single-stringed instrument, here correctly shown being bowed above the point of touching. The first accounts of this instrument are in German sources, and are no earlier than the beginning of the sixteenth century. The German name is *Trumscheit* ("drum-log"), and the later term "marina" has no satisfactory explanation. Little music for the instrument was written down. One instance is the use of two tromba marinas which echo two muted trumpets in a scene of Alessandro Scarlatti's opera *Mitridate Eupatore* (1707), at a time when there was some revival of interest in this curious instrument.

LXII   *Tromba Marina*

63

The *PSALTERY* consists of a flat soundbox above which the strings run horizontally. The still current Near Eastern form *Canun* is played with plectra attached to the fingers. From the tenth century onwards it spread to Western Europe, where it appeared in various forms, the most usual being the pig-headed shape (*Istromento di porco*). Medieval iconography showed it held against the chest, a device for making its shape clear, or on the knees, which was the true playing position. In Europe it was played either with goose-quill plectra or with the fingers.

LXIII   *Salterio Turchesco*

64

When an instrument of the psaltery type is played with beaters (here of cane) it is generally known as a *DULCIMER*. The idea may have come in the first place from Persia. The Italians, among whom it seems to have been little known, called the instrument *salterio tedesco* ("German psaltery"), while its German name is *Hackbrett* ("chopping board"). The most developed form is the Hungarian and Roumanian *cimbalon*, which is played with great virtuosity and brio. Liszt transferred many of its characteristic effects to the piano, and Kodály has used the instrument itself in his *Háry János* suite.

LXIV *Salterio Tedesco*

65

Unlike many medieval instruments, the *HURDY-GURDY* seems to have been invented in Europe, not brought from the Near East. When the Abbot Odo of Cluny wrote instructions for making it, by the name *organistrum*, in the tenth century, it was probably used for rehearsing plainsong. Pictures in the twelfth century show it as a large instrument, one person turning the wheel which acted as a mechanical bow, another working the rods which stopped the strings. In the thirteenth century it became a one-man portable instrument, called *symphonia* in Latin, *simphonie* in French. Later it descended to a rustic and mendicants' instrument, especially in Germany, and as such was taken up by fashionable society in France as part of the "back to nature" movement. Haydn wrote concertos and *notturni* for the eighteenth-century form, called the *lira organizzata*. It is still made in the Auvergne, where it flourishes in popular bands with fiddle, *cabrette* (bagpipe) and accordion.

LXV *Lira Tedesca*

66

Bonanni says that the *HARP* "is not much played in Italy but a great deal in Germany," though he seems to have been unaware of contemporary German experiments in the direction of mechanisation. These, starting with rather clumsy manually operated hooks which changed the pitch of the strings, had produced by 1720 a simple pedal harp, with the pitch-changing apparatus worked by the feet as in the modern harp. The plate shows clearly the large four-sided sound box of the pre-pedal harp. This is found now only in some of the rustic instruments of South America, which are still made in the style of seventeenth-century Spanish harps.

LXVI   *Arpa*

67

The *VIOLIN* seems to have been a professional instrument from its first appearance in the mid-sixteenth century, when its unfretted finger-board, vivid tone color, large dynamic range and generally lively character differentiated it strongly from the gentler and less mobile viols. Mersenne had commented on its versatility in having the power of the lute to suggest sadness and also the liveliness of the trumpet, and Bonanni remarks that its sound is *molto acuto*, very sharp. It is unique in having come in nearly perfect form from the hands of its unknown creators, and the earliest surviving specimens (made by Andrea Amati, *c*. 1505–1580 and Gasparo da Salò, 1540–1609) are still among the finest. Antonio Stradivari, the most famous of all makers, was contemporary with Bonanni, as were Corelli and Vivaldi. Besides the art fiddling represented then by the sonatas for solo violin and the *concerti grossi* for massed strings of these and other composers, there were, and indeed still are, old and vigorous rustic fiddle traditions in many parts of Europe.

109

LXVII   *Violino*

68

The earliest known use of the term viol d'amore is in Evelyn's *Diary* for 1679. He enjoyed "for its sweetnesse and novelty, the viol d'amore of 5 wyre-strings plaid with a bow." Nine years later the German Daniel Speer described it as having double steel or gut strings, clearly implying the use of sympathetic strings, which became a characteristic feature of the *VIOLA D'AMORE* of the following century. In its final form it had a secondary set of wire strings lying under the six bowed gut strings. Joseph Majer in 1741 said that there were two sizes, one like a violin, the other larger than a viola. Bonanni's description, which has the heading *Viola d'Amore*, corroborates the use of sympathetic strings, while his plate, with the caption *Violino d'Amore*, depicts the violin-shaped instrument without sympathetic strings (the position of the bow is, of course, impossible, and the peg-box appears to have six pegs). Praetorius had observed that a violin with metal strings had a calm and lovely tone. It seems likely that the viola d'amore for which Ariosti wrote sonatas, and which Bach included in two beautiful contemplative movements of the St. John Passion, was a wire-strung violin type, not the large and elaborate viola d'amore.

LXVIII   *Violino di Amore*

69

The *SPIKE-FIDDLE* is not only Turkish, but is found in all Islamic countries from Siam to North Africa. The sound-box is covered with a parchment diaphragm, and the long protrusion, which has the same function as the spike of the cello, is the feature from which it takes its Western name.

Violino Turchesco

70

The instruments in this plate and the next were taken from illustrations of Persian instruments in a travel book by Engelbert Kempfer. In fact, both of them are of non-Persian origin. This simplified form of the Chinese zither *tseng*, which Kempfer called *TSJENG*, probably reached Persia, along with other foreign instruments, in the sixteenth century. Although Kempfer's plate did not show it being played, his text clearly implied its playing position, which is flat, like all the zither family. Bonanni's engraver has copied the fiddle-like peg-box, which is somewhat inaccurate, from Kempfer, and given it a guitar-like playing position.

Salterio Persiano

71

The instrument which Kempfer called "a four-stringed foreign pandura played with a bow" was the Indian *SARINDA*, a short fiddle. His text again made the playing position, which was downwards like a 'cello, perfectly clear. The engraver has simplified its appearance here and has placed it like a European violin.

Violino Persiano

72

This is meant to be the ancient *FRAME DRUM*, a large jingle-less tambourine. It was used chiefly by women dancers and appears in the Bible as *tympanum*. The bells which surround the frame in this picture are a misrepresentation of the protruding heads of the nails which fastened the skin to the frame.

LXXII   *Timpano antico*

73

The *TAMBOURINE* with jingles let into the frame appeared in Europe in the thirteenth century. It came, like so many medieval instruments, from the Near East during the Crusades.

Timpano Moderno

74

The *MILITARY SIDE DRUM* was developed from the fourteenth century onwards as a functional instrument for the new mercenary foot soldiers, who marched to its loud and incisive beat. The German military fife and drum ensembles were famous all over Europe, and Bonanni says that the drum used in Germany was larger than that used in Italy.

LXXIV   *Tamburro Militare*

75

LARGE KETTLEDRUMS, played on horse- or camel-back in Ottoman military bands, were known in Eastern Europe for some time before they reached the West towards the end of the fifteenth century. Their imposing sonority made them exclusively aristocratic instruments, and although they were played with trumpets in the first place, by the end of the seventeenth century elaborate music was being written for three or four kettledrums alone, and they began to be used in orchestral as well as military and ceremonial music.

Timballi

76

Small kettledrums, or NAKERS, came to the West from the Islamic world two centuries earlier than the large cavalry kettledrums. Bonanni's illustration is taken from a plate showing a Turkish bride arriving at her husband's house, attended by a drummer beating on two nakers hung from the shoulders of a servant.

Timballo Turchesco

77

This picture of a primitive *TUBULAR DRUM*, with one head at the
end of a hollowed-out tree trunk, was made from a description given
by the Capuchin monk, Fortunato Alamandini. It is found in the south
Pacific and Central America as well as on the east and west coasts of
Africa.

Tamburro Affricano

78

Two Indonesian drums are described in the text accompanying this made-up illustration. One is of scooped-out wood. The other is a *GOURD DRUM* with little bells hanging from the head. It is beaten with a stick.

LXXVIII   *Tamburro Affricano*

79

The *BARREL DRUM*, of which this is a small Persian example, is found from the Middle to the Far East. The smaller barrel drums are played with the hands, this technique reaching its highest degree of complication in India. The larger drums found in the Far East are played with sticks.

Tamburro Persiano

80

This *DRUM* with a long resonating tube was a suggestion of Kircher, who believed that it would have an imposing and far-carrying sound.

LXXX   *Tubo Timpanite*

81

It seems likely that this is meant to be the Chinese *RESTING BELL* (*shun*), an upturned basin of bronze which is struck on the rim with a metal hammer.

119

LXXXI   *Tamburro Cinese*

82

A Lappish *SHAMAN DRUM*, single-sided and beaten with a bone hammer. On the membrane, which is painted with scarlet figures, lies a chained metal tongue. When the drum is beaten the tongue jumps and the future is divined from its position.

Tamburro Lapponico

83

The *FRICTION DRUM* consists of a vessel of pottery or wood with a skin head containing a central perforation into which a stick fits. The drum, which makes a rumbling noise not unlike a bullfrog, is sounded by rubbing the stick up and down in the hole. Its origin is not known. It is associated with fertility rites in primitive communities, while in Europe it is a humble fiesta and fairground instrument.

LXXXIII   *Inſtrumento nelle Vendemmie*

84

The *SISTRUM*, like the aulos, was used for several thousand years among ancient Mediterranean peoples. In Egypt it was associated with the rites of certain deities such as Hathor and Isis and their symbols often appear on the instruments. This illustration was probably taken from Mersenne, where the sacred cat on top of the sistrum and the snake-headed jingling rods appear in rather clearer detail than in this plate. The instrument is still used in the Coptic Church, and simpler forms exist in West Africa, Malaya and North and South America.

LXXXIV   *Sistro*

85

The *TRIANGLE* was not always triangular in shape when it first appeared in the fifteenth century, and it was known by many names. Mersenne called it *cymbale* and Praetorius "*crotalum*, vulgo ein Triangel." Until the nineteenth century it carried several jingling rings on the lower bar. Bonanni incorrectly shows five bars with rings, having confused it with the sistrum and crotalum (see Plates 84 and 89).

Crotalo

86

Cymbals were introduced into ancient Greece from Asia with the rites of Oriental deities. The plate shows *CUP-SHAPED CYMBALS*, which have no equivalent in Western European music, though they appear in some early medieval drawings after antique models.

LXXXVI   *Cembalo Antico*

*8*7

These are the *SMALL CYMBALS* which were used by *cymbalistriae*, women dancers at the feasts of Bacchus. Cymbals of this size are occasionally represented in Western medieval paintings.

Cembalo diuerſo

88

The Armenians accompanied the chants of an important Mass with *FLAT CYMBALS*. Less concave in shape than antique cymbals, they were held by strings passing through their centers.

Cembalo dell'Armeno

89

The Greek term *krotalon* covered all kinds of small clappers. The Maronites and Armenians, says Bonanni, used small cymbal clappers in their services. He then goes on to describe *ELEVATION BELLS* attached to a circular frame used by the Syrians to signal the Elevation of the Host at Mass (see Plate 132). These, of course, have nothing to do with clappers.

LXXXIX *Crotalo degl'Armeni*

90

In the rites of the Armenians groups of the kind of cymbals shown in
Plate 88 were sounded, together with a shallow cup-shaped *TONGUE-
LESS BELL* which was struck by an iron bar.

128

XC   *Instrumento Sacro degl'Armeni*

91

This African *DOUBLE BELL*, tuned to two different notes, is made of iron and is beaten with a wooden stick. It is familiar now from its use in Afro-Caribbean music, but it was known only from travellers' tales in Bonanni's day.

XCI   *Instrumento Affricano*

92

An African *SINGLE BELL* which Bonanni describes as "like that which in Italy is hung from the necks of cattle, but square in shape."

XCII   *Altro Instrumento Affricano*

93

The *CASTANETS*, two pieces of hollowed out hardwood held and clicked together in one hand, are the only Western survivor of the self-manipulated instruments of the dancers of antiquity.

Baccante con Nacchera

94

Tiny FINGER CYMBALS attached to the thumbs and forefingers were used by the dancers of antiquity. Bonanni observes that Coptic priests use them to accompany the chanting of prayers, and that the sound of many finger cymbals being clashed together fills the church.

XCIV *Inſtrumento delli Cofti*

95

Bonanni's authority for attributing these *WOODEN CLAPPERS*, which he calls castanets, to Turkey, is a passage in the writings of Ottavio Ferrari, from whom he also took the illustration.

Gnacchare delli Turchi

96

Children use for clappers such basic materials as pieces of china, *STONES*, *BONES*, shells and suchlike.

XCVI   *Instrumenti Fanciulleschi*

97

The *JEW'S HARP*, or Jaw's Harp, is widely distributed among primitive and civilised peoples. At its simplest it is a strip of bamboo cut in the shape of a comb with only one tooth; when made in metal, the tooth, or tongue, is a separate piece soldered to the frame. In each case the instrument is set between the player's teeth, and the mouth cavity amplifies the sound made by plucking the free tongue of the "harp." It is essentially an instrument for the player's pleasure, being hardly audible to anyone else.

XCVII   *Spassa Pensiere*

98

The *XYLOPHONE* appears in primitive and sophisticated form in Africa and all over the Far East. It is first mentioned in Europe in the sixteenth century and Holbein's *Dance of Death* woodcuts include one of Death playing a xylophone. Mersenne describes it as a practice instrument for carillon players and Bonanni says it is much used in Tuscany. It was an itinerant's instrument until the middle of the nineteenth century, since when, in larger form, it has joined the orchestral tuned percussion.

XCVIII   *Zilorgano*

99

The effects of music have been observed, says Bonanni, on fish, birds and bees. His engraving shows a bee-keeper recalling the swarm to the hive by striking on a large metal vessel.

Instrumento per le Api

A large *GONG* used in Indonesia to summon the people for official proclamations.

C. *Tamburro di Batam*

101

Traditionally called a *GONG CHIME* in English, but now more frequently referred to as *TUNED KETTLES*, this instrument is peculiar
to Southeast Asia. It is one of the great array of tuned percussions in
wood, metal or bamboo, which form the main part of the ensembles of
Indonesia. The illustration, which seems to be taken from a source
also used by Praetorius, shows flat, cymbal-like plates instead of the
kettles with high central bosses.

CI   *Instrumento in Batam*

A set of *SUSPENDED GONGS*, apparently taken from the same source. Praetorius called them "American," but Bonanni attributes them correctly to Indonesia.

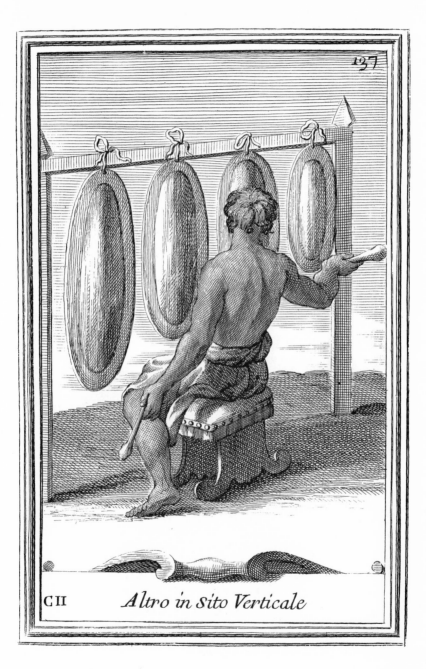

CII   *Altro in Sito Verticale*

103

The uses of *BELLS* are innumerable and pervade every aspect of life. This engraving shows a particularly grim one—a criminal being exposed to public scorn with a bell hung about his neck. The second engraving shows bells of different kinds which were preserved in the Kircher Museum in the Jesuit College in Rome. Besides discussing the ritual and social uses of bells, Bonanni is interested in their size, citing correctly the world's largest bell as the Czar's bell in Moscow, which weighs about 198 tons.

Campanello del Reo

138

104

This shows the manner of carrying and striking a *SMALL BELL* in processions of the Western Church.

Campanello del Clero

105

This shows another way of carrying a bell in processions. A large bell suspended in a wooden turret on wheels is said to have been devised in Cremona in the eleventh century. This form of *PROCESSIONAL BELL* was used to give signals to companies of troops, a function later discharged by the trumpet.

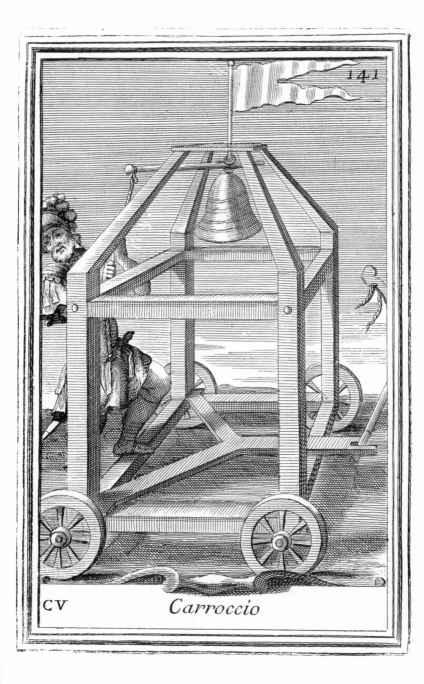

141

CV   *Carroccio*

106

The *CARILLON* was developed in the Netherlands. About the year 1500 bells were played from a keyboard, and a century later a pedal-board was added. Evelyn tells in his *Diary* of going to the carillon in the tower of St. Nicholas' Church in Amsterdam, and seeing "one who played all sorts of compositions from the tablature before him, as if he had fingered an organ." He observed that "it was impossible for the musician, or any that stood near him, to hear anything himself; yet to those at a distance, and especially in the streets, the harmony and the time were most exact and agreeable." Bonanni refers to the carillon at Liège, which had thirty-three bells. Among notable carillons today are those at Riverside Church in New York, at the University of Michigan, and in the Peace Tower at Ottawa.

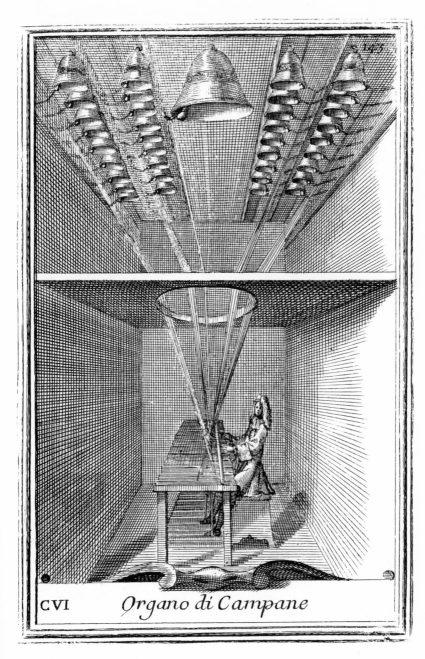

CVI   *Organo di Campane*

107

This is a *RUSTIC BELL* like that hung from the collars of cattle. It was used by the crowd at carnival time to mock or applaud the maskers. It was also rung in Rome by groups who drove around in carriages to celebrate the award of a doctorate to one of their number. Bonanni expresses some satisfaction that this custom, so unsuited to the dignity of the degree, has recently been forbidden by the university on pain of a fine of fifty scudi.

144

CVII   *Campanaccio del Villano*

108

This is a notion of Kircher's to demonstrate an acoustical effect. A metal bar is suspended by a thick gut string held to the ears. The sound of the bar being struck by a metal rod should seem to the hearer like the tolling of a very large bell.

CVIII · *Verga di Metallo*

109

Though bells were used in the Western Church from early times, they were not known in the Greek Church before the eleventh century. The Greek churches used the *SEMANTERION* ("sign giver") which is depicted here. It consisted of a wooden plank which was struck with two mallets in such a way as to give distinct musical sounds. This size was suspended by a string held between the teeth.

CIX. *Campana delli Greci*

110

The *SMALL SEMANTERION* was struck with an iron hammer, as seen in this plate. There was also a very large size which was hung from a tower.

CX   *Altra Simile*

III

This shows the form of *WOODEN SEMANTERION* used in the Coptic Church.

Legno delli Cofti

112

This brings us to the use of noise-makers in the Western Church. During the three days before Easter (Maundy Thursday, Good Friday and Holy Saturday) the sound of bells is banned, and *RATTLES* are used instead. This kind had iron knockers which struck against the wooden boards when the latter were turned back and forth. The Capuchins used this device regularly to summon the monks to Matins, which begins before dawn. The same type of rattle is still found in Corsica, and was also used by Russian police.

CXII   *Crepitacolo per le Chiese*

113

A *BOX RATTLE* used in the Western Church. K. P. Wachsmann has observed that in primitive cultures rattles "often have a magico-religious significance and are frequently part of the equipment of the witch-doctor" (*Musical Instruments through the Ages*, ed. A. Baines). Bonanni's selection of examples illustrates well the ritual and other social functions of noise-makers of various kinds.

CXIII   *Altro diuerso*

114

A *LARGE RATTLE* used in Holy Week in Spain and Mexico. It was placed in a bell tower and could be heard over a great distance.

CXIV   *Matracca*

115

A *TOY WHEEL* used by children in Flanders. Small bells were attached to the rim.

CXV   *Rota Fiammenga*

116

A noise-maker used by country folk in Tuscany. It consisted of a *WOODEN POT* which was struck rhythmically by a wooden beater made in the form of a pestle.

CXVI   *Bacioccolo*

117

In Holy Week young boys amused themselves with rattles of various kinds, such as the *TRIC-TRAC*. Sometimes they even sounded them in church to mock the ritual rattles—as one might expect, to the great annoyance of the worshippers.

CXVII   *Fanciullo con Trich Trach*

118

This boy is using a familiar noise-maker, a *COG RATTLE*. In Corsica this kind of rattle, unlike the knocker type shown in Plate 112, could be sounded in church by any worshipper.

CXVIII *Fanciullo con Trich Trach*

119

Here are two *TOY RATTLES*. The one in the baby's left hand has a cover made of skin at each end and is filled with small stones. This is like the primitive "rattle drum." The other is a small rattle consisting of a bell inside a woven basket globe. This is like the primitive "basket rattle."

CXIX   *Altro diuerſo uſato dalle Nutrici*

Although Bonanni says this *XYLOPHONE* is used in Batavia, the description of its musical context, with a chorus of men and women and leaping dancers, seems to suggest Africa, as the title indicates.

CXX   *Instrumento Africano*

121

The picture is formalised but the text gives an exact description of the *MARIMBA*, saying it is the sweetest and most agreeable of all African instruments. These delicately tuned xylophones, with a gourd resonator to each wood block, were taken by slaves to South America and finally evolved into the large instrument which is now part of the orchestral percussionist's kit.

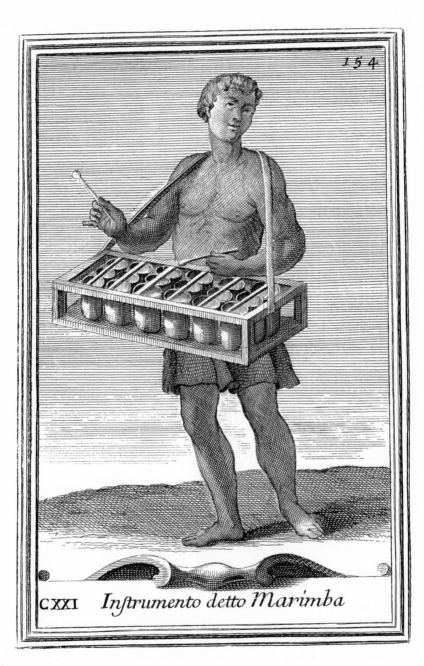

154

CXXI *Inſtrumento detto Marimba*

122

Bonanni took the Indian *VINA* from Mersenne who described it correctly as a stick body with two gourd resonators, movable frets, and five strings plucked by the thumb and by the fingertips furnished with metal plectra. He gave, however, only one string in his illustration, merely marking the placing of pegs for the others, and the engraver has taken it to be a single string instrument played with beaters.

CXXII   *Instrumento Indiano*

123

This is the Neapolitan folk instrument *TRICCHE-BALLACCHE*. It has three or five wooden hammers, that in the centre being fixed while the others are moved laterally to strike against it and, in the type with five hammers, against each other.

Trich Varlach

124

Bonanni speaks slightingly of *MARACAS*, gourds filled with stones and shaken rhythmically, used by "savages who know no better instrument."

CXXIV   *Instrumento di Affricani*

125

STRUNG RATTLES of nut shell are fixed to the arms and legs of this Brazilian dancer. They make a noise like the "jingles which in Italy are attached to the feet of horses or dancers."

CXXV   *Donna Brasiliana in ballo*

126

A *RATTLE* from India made of metal jingles in the shape of a crown. It is thrown from one hand to the other by dancers, and "makes an agreeable sound to the ears of the barbarians who are accustomed to it." Bonanni is generally scornful of rhythm instruments which have no accepted classical ancestry.

CXXVI   *Instrumento del Madurè*

127

The *KROUPALON* (Latin *scabellum*), or percussive wooden-soled shoe of the leader of the Greek chorus, was a device for setting and stabilising rhythm. A vestige of it survives in the stamping foot of Scottish and Irish bagpipers.

CXXVII   *Scabillo degl' Antichi*

BEGGAR'S CLAPPERS. In the Middle Ages clappers were also used by lepers as a warning of their presence.

156

CXXVIII   *Crotalo del Mendico*

129

The Franciscans used as a *MONASTIC ALARM* a piece of wood cut into many strips, with which they beat on the door of each cell.

CXXIX *Religioso Suegliatore*

130

Another of the many ways of signalling to monks. The Capuchins, who lay great stress on poverty, summoned the community to meals by striking a board with a stick of knotty wood.

CXXX. *Tauola percossa dal Cappuccino*

131

A coachman's *WHIP*.

CXXXI *Frusta del Cocchiero*

132

This form of the *ELEVATION BELL* at Mass consists of a suspended wheel turned from below by means of a cord.

163

Sonagli adoprati nella Chiesa

133

Here three *WOODEN SPOONS* are used as noise-makers, two being held in the left hand, one in the right. Bonanni says that they are used at harvesting time by rough peasants, who have no other way of accompanying their songs.

CXXXIII *Cucchiari di legno*

134

FALCON DRUMS are tiny kettle drums, hung from the waist. They are used by Persian falconers to call the preying birds back to the wrist.

Timballi Perfiani

135

A *SWORD BLADE* beaten with iron tips attached to the fingers of the right hand is said by Bonanni to be played in the streets of Naples by the common people, and to make a most pleasant sound. A sword blade is beaten during the Christmas Mass in some remote village churches in the Balearics.

CXXXV   *Spada percossa*

136

This illustration was made up from a vague description of an instrument which was played with drums when the Chinese Emperor appeared in public. Few precise accounts of Chinese signal instruments exist, and it is difficult to identify this instrument, and that given in Plate 141, with any exactitude.

C.XXXVI   *Instrumento Cinese*

137

This is the *BASS DRUM* or "big drum" depicted (much too small) as a Turkish instrument, as indeed it was when the engraving was made. About the middle of the eighteenth century it was introduced into European military bands. "Turkish music" quickly became popular, and we find it in Haydn's *Military Symphony* and in Mozart's *Abduction from the Seraglio*. Western drummers, however, are singularly reluctant to use the Turkish manner of beating with a stick on one side and a switch or cane on the other.

CXXXVII *Tamburro sonato dal Turco*

138

The free-reed mouth organ, sounded by suction as well as by blowing, which is called *SHENG* in China and *SHO* in Japan, has a recorded history of more than three thousand years. A classical instrument in both these countries, it is also found in rougher form all over the Far East. It is likely that interest in its construction started the experiments which led to the invention of the European concertina, accordion, harmonium and harmonica.

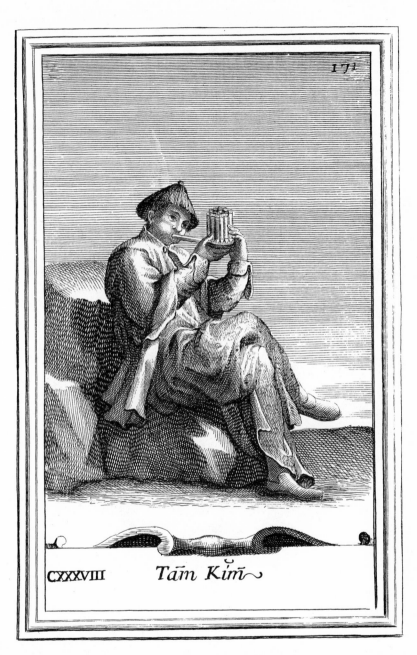

CXXXVIII   *Tām Kĭm*

139

The Chinese suspended *GONG CHIME* (*yün lo*) has ten small gongs, not twelve as the plate shows. It was used in the Imperial court, but it is now one of the lesser instruments of China, generally poorly tuned and inexpertly played.

CXXXIX   *Altro Stromento Cinese*

140

Small *CUP-SHAPED CYMBALS* go by the name of *Tiè Zù* in China, according to Bonanni. The picture is of an Indian courtesan dancing with a similar instrument (see Plate 86).

CXL   * Tiè Zù*

141

This picture was made up from a description given by the Dutch ambassador to China. The clapper of a *BELL* held in the left hand was activated by the ridges on a wooden cylinder hung from the neck and turned by the right hand.

CXLI   *Altro Istromento Cinese*

142

Although Bonanni says that a "*CYMBAL*" of this kind was preserved in the Museum of the Jesuit College, it is an unlikely instrument as he describes it—a metal plate with a hole in the center, hung around with small bells.

Altro Cembalo antico

143

A *TRUMPET* made of coiled bark, decorated with rings from which hang metal discs, used by the Indians of Florida.

174

CXLIII   *Tromba della Florida*

144

The African *SANSA* consists of a number of thin iron or cane tongues, sometimes with metal shakers attached, which are fixed over a gourd or wood resonator so that one end of the tongue is free. These free ends are pushed down by the thumbs and forefingers and the resulting sound is delicate and ethereal. The sansa existed in its present form at least four hundred years ago, for it was described in travellers' tales in the late sixteenth century.

CXLIV   *Marimba de Cafri*

145

This African *MUSICAL BOW* is sounded by a swan-feather beater, weighted with lead or wood and decorated with rings and jingles. Pressure from the player's thumb on the string alters the fundamental pitch. No resonator is shown in the plate, though a musical bow is almost inaudible without one.

CXLV   *Arco de Cafri*

146

Bowed instruments were found in Negro Africa only where there had been Arab influence or infiltration. This is meant to be the Arab *SPIKE-FIDDLE*, with skin-covered gourd body and only one string. It is held downwards, not upwards as shown in the plate.

CXLVI *Violino de Cafri*

147

A *RATTLE* made of a hollow seed-filled gourd was used, according to Bonanni's source, in the solemn feasts of the Indians of Virginia. It was accompanied by the beating of sticks on stones.

CXLVII   *Zucca*

148

This *GILDED BRASS BALL* is probably that mentioned by Vicenzo Giustiniani in his *Discorso sopra la Musica* about a century before Bonanni's work. It was invented, Giustiniani said, by a Bolognese gold-smith Francesco Tunnilla, and enclosed machinery which made a delightful sound when the ball was moved. Bonanni tells us that it was dismantled by a certain Monsignor Leone Strozzi, who was eager to see what made the intriguing sound. It turned out to be what we should describe as a rather complicated maraca (see Plate 124). Inside the outer casing were two balls each cut in half and provided with teeth. Inside of all was a small complete ball. "With this," says Bonanni, "we close our Gabinetto."

Palla di Bronzo

CXLVIII

Index

A CATALOGUE OF SELECTED DOVER BOOKS
IN ALL FIELDS OF INTEREST

THE NOTEBOOKS OF LEONARDO DA VINCI, edited by J.P. Richter. Extracts from manuscripts reveal great genius; on painting, sculpture, anatomy, sciences, geography, etc. Both Italian and English. 186 ms. pages reproduced, plus 500 additional drawings, including studies for Last Supper, Sforza monument, etc. 860pp. 7⅞ x 10¾.   USO 22572-0, 22573-9 Pa., Two vol. set $15.90

ART NOUVEAU DESIGNS IN COLOR, Alphonse Mucha, Maurice Verneuil, Georges Auriol. Full-color reproduction of Combinaisons ornamentales (c. 1900) by Art Nouveau masters. Floral, animal, geometric, interlacings, swashes — borders, frames, spots — all incredibly beautiful. 60 plates, hundreds of designs. 9⅜ x 8¹/₁₆.   22885-1 Pa. $4.00

GRAPHIC WORKS OF ODILON REDON. All great fantastic lithographs, etchings, engravings, drawings, 209 in all. Monsters, Huysmans, still life work, etc. Introduction by Alfred Werner. 209pp. 9⅛ x 12¼.   21996-8 Pa. $6.00

EXOTIC FLORAL PATTERNS IN COLOR, E.-A. Seguy. Incredibly beautiful full-color pochoir work by great French designer of 20's. Complete Bouquets et frondaisons, Suggestions pour étoffes. Richness must be seen to be believed. 40 plates containing 120 patterns. 80pp. 9⅜ x 12¼.   23041-4 Pa. $6.00

SELECTED ETCHINGS OF JAMES A. McN. WHISTLER, James A. McN. Whistler. 149 outstanding etchings by the great American artist, including selections from the Thames set and two Venice sets, the complete French set, and many individual prints. Introduction and explanatory note on each print by Maria Naylor. 157pp. 9⅜ x 12¼.   23194-1 Pa. $5.00

VISUAL ILLUSIONS: THEIR CAUSES, CHARACTERISTICS, AND APPLICATIONS, Matthew Luckiesh. Thorough description, discussion; shape and size, color, motion; natural illusion. Uses in art and industry. 100 illustrations. 252pp.
21530-X Pa. $3.00

TEN BOOKS ON ARCHITECTURE, Vitruvius. The most important book ever written on architecture. Early Roman aesthetics, technology, classical orders, site selection, all other aspects. Stands behind everything since. Morgan translation. 331pp.
20645-9 Pa. $3.75

THE CODEX NUTTALL, A PICTURE MANUSCRIPT FROM ANCIENT MEXICO, as first edited by Zelia Nuttall. Only inexpensive edition, in full color, of a pre-Columbian Mexican (Mixtec) book. 88 color plates show kings, gods, heroes, temples, sacrifices. New explanatory, historical introduction by Arthur G. Miller. 96pp. 11⅜ x 8½.   23168-2 Pa. $7.50

CREATIVE LITHOGRAPHY AND HOW TO DO IT, Grant Arnold. Lithography as art form: working directly on stone, transfer of drawings, lithotint, mezzotint, color printing; also metal plates. Detailed, thorough. 27 illustrations. 214pp.
21208-4 Pa. $3.50

DESIGN MOTIFS OF ANCIENT MEXICO, Jorge Enciso. Vigorous, powerful ceramic stamp impressions — Maya, Aztec, Toltec, Olmec. Serpents, gods, priests, dancers, etc. 153pp. 6⅛ x 9¼. 20084-1 Pa. $2.50

AMERICAN INDIAN DESIGN AND DECORATION, Leroy Appleton. Full text, plus more than 700 precise drawings of Inca, Maya, Aztec, Pueblo, Plains, NW Coast basketry, sculpture, painting, pottery, sand paintings, metal, etc. 4 plates in color. 279pp. 8⅜ x 11¼. 22704-9 Pa.$5.00

CHINESE LATTICE DESIGNS, Daniel S. Dye. Incredibly beautiful geometric designs: circles, voluted, simple dissections, etc. Inexhaustible source of ideas, motifs. 1239 illustrations. 469pp. 6⅛ x 9¼. 23096-1 Pa. $5.00

JAPANESE DESIGN MOTIFS, Matsuya Co. Mon, or heraldic designs. Over 4000 typical, beautiful designs: birds, animals, flowers, swords, fans, geometric; all beautifully stylized. 213pp. 11⅜ x 8¼. 22874-6 Pa. $5.00

PERSPECTIVE, Jan Vredeman de Vries. 73 perspective plates from 1604 edition; buildings, townscapes, stairways, fantastic scenes. Remarkable for beauty, surrealistic atmosphere; real eye-catchers. Introduction by Adolf Placzek. 74pp. 11⅜ x 8¼. 20186-4 Pa. $3.00

EARLY AMERICAN DESIGN MOTIFS, Suzanne E. Chapman. 497 motifs, designs, from painting on wood, ceramics, appliqué, glassware, samplers, metal work, etc. Florals, landscapes, birds and animals, geometrics, letters, etc. Inexhaustible. Enlarged edition. 138pp. 8⅜ x 11¼. 22985-8 Pa. $3.50
23084-8 Clothbd. $7.95

VICTORIAN STENCILS FOR DESIGN AND DECORATION, edited by E.V. Gillon, Jr. 113 wonderful ornate Victorian pieces from German sources; florals, geometrics; borders, corner pieces; bird motifs, etc. 64pp. 9⅜ x 12¼. 21995-X Pa. $3.00

ART NOUVEAU: AN ANTHOLOGY OF DESIGN AND ILLUSTRATION FROM THE STUDIO, edited by E.V. Gillon, Jr. Graphic arts: book jackets, posters, engravings, illustrations, decorations; Crane, Beardsley, Bradley and many others. Inexhaustible. 92pp. 8⅛ x 11. 22388-4 Pa. $2.50

ORIGINAL ART DECO DESIGNS, William Rowe. First-rate, highly imaginative modern Art Deco frames, borders, compositions, alphabets, florals, insectals, Wurlitzer-types, etc. Much finest modern Art Deco. 80 plates, 8 in color. 8⅜ x 11¼. 22567-4 Pa. $3.50

HANDBOOK OF DESIGNS AND DEVICES, Clarence P. Hornung. Over 1800 basic geometric designs based on circle, triangle, square, scroll, cross, etc. Largest such collection in existence. 261pp. 20125-2 Pa. $2.75

150 MASTERPIECES OF DRAWING, edited by Anthony Toney. 150 plates, early 15th century to end of 18th century; Rembrandt, Michelangelo, Dürer, Fragonard, Watteau, Wouwerman, many others. 150pp. 8⅜ x 11¼.   21032-4 Pa. $4.00

THE GOLDEN AGE OF THE POSTER, Hayward and Blanche Cirker. 70 extraordinary posters in full colors, from Maîtres de l'Affiche, Mucha, Lautrec, Bradley, Cheret, Beardsley, many others. 9⅜ x 12¼.   22753-7 Pa. $5.95

SIMPLICISSIMUS, selection, translations and text by Stanley Appelbaum. 180 satirical drawings, 16 in full color, from the famous German weekly magazine in the years 1896 to 1926. 24 artists included: Grosz, Kley, Pascin, Kubin, Kollwitz, plus Heine, Thöny, Bruno Paul, others. 172pp. 8½ x 12¼.   23098-8 Pa. $5.00
23099-6 Clothbd. $10.00

THE EARLY WORK OF AUBREY BEARDSLEY, Aubrey Beardsley. 157 plates, 2 in color: Manon Lescaut, Madame Bovary, Morte d'Arthur, Salome, other. Introduction by H. Marillier. 175pp. 8½ x 11.   21816-3 Pa. $4.00

THE LATER WORK OF AUBREY BEARDSLEY, Aubrey Beardsley. Exotic masterpieces of full maturity: Venus and Tannhäuser, Lysistrata, Rape of the Lock, Volpone, Savoy material, etc. 174 plates, 2 in color. 176pp. 8½ x 11.   21817-1 Pa. $4.50

DRAWINGS OF WILLIAM BLAKE, William Blake. 92 plates from Book of Job, Divine Comedy, Paradise Lost, visionary heads, mythological figures, Laocoön, etc. Selection, introduction, commentary by Sir Geoffrey Keynes. 178pp. 8½ x 11.
22303-5 Pa. $4.00

LONDON: A PILGRIMAGE, Gustave Doré, Blanchard Jerrold. Squalor, riches, misery, beauty of mid-Victorian metropolis; 55 wonderful plates, 125 other illustrations, full social, cultural text by Jerrold. 191pp. of text. 8⅛ x 11.
22306-X Pa. $6.00

THE COMPLETE WOODCUTS OF ALBRECHT DÜRER, edited by Dr. W. Kurth. 346 in all: Old Testament, St. Jerome, Passion, Life of Virgin, Apocalypse, many others. Introduction by Campbell Dodgson. 285pp. 8½ x 12¼.   21097-9 Pa. $6.00

THE DISASTERS OF WAR, Francisco Goya. 83 etchings record horrors of Napoleonic wars in Spain and war in general. Reprint of 1st edition, plus 3 additional plates. Introduction by Philip Hofer. 97pp. 9⅜ x 8¼.   21872-4 Pa. $3.50

ENGRAVINGS OF HOGARTH, William Hogarth. 101 of Hogarth's greatest works: Rake's Progress, Harlot's Progress, Illustrations for Hudibras, Midnight Modern Conversation, Before and After, Beer Street and Gin Lane, many more. Full commentary. 256pp. 11 x 14.   22479-1 Pa. $7.95

PRIMITIVE ART, Franz Boas. Great anthropologist on ceramics, textiles, wood, stone, metal, etc.; patterns, technology, symbols, styles. All areas, but fullest on Northwest Coast Indians. 350 illustrations. 378pp.   20025-6 Pa. $3.75

MOTHER GOOSE'S MELODIES. Facsimile of fabulously rare Munroe and Francis "copyright 1833" Boston edition. Familiar and unusual rhymes, wonderful old woodcut illustrations. Edited by E.F. Bleiler. 128pp. 4½ x 6⅜. 22577-1 Pa. $1.50

MOTHER GOOSE IN HIEROGLYPHICS. Favorite nursery rhymes presented in rebus form for children. Fascinating 1849 edition reproduced in toto, with key. Introduction by E.F. Bleiler. About 400 woodcuts. 64pp. 6⅞ x 5¼. 20745-5 Pa. $1.50

PETER PIPER'S PRACTICAL PRINCIPLES OF PLAIN & PERFECT PRONUNCIATION. Alliterative jingles and tongue-twisters. Reproduction in full of 1830 first American edition. 25 spirited woodcuts. 32pp. 4½ x 6⅜. 22560-7 Pa. $1.25

MARMADUKE MULTIPLY'S MERRY METHOD OF MAKING MINOR MATHEMATICIANS. Fellow to Peter Piper, it teaches multiplication table by catchy rhymes and woodcuts. 1841 Munroe & Francis edition. Edited by E.F. Bleiler. 103pp. 4⅝ x 6. 22773-1 Pa. $1.25

THE NIGHT BEFORE CHRISTMAS, Clement Moore. Full text, and woodcuts from original 1848 book. Also critical, historical material. 19 illustrations. 40pp. 4⅝ x 6. 22797-9 Pa. $1.35

THE KING OF THE GOLDEN RIVER, John Ruskin. Victorian children's classic of three brothers, their attempts to reach the Golden River, what becomes of them. Facsimile of original 1889 edition. 22 illustrations. 56pp. 4⅝ x 6⅜. 20066-3 Pa. $1.50

DREAMS OF THE RAREBIT FIEND, Winsor McCay. Pioneer cartoon strip, unexcelled for beauty, imagination, in 60 full sequences. Incredible technical virtuosity, wonderful visual wit. Historical introduction. 62pp. 8⅜ x 11¼. 21347-1 Pa. $2.50

THE KATZENJAMMER KIDS, Rudolf Dirks. In full color, 14 strips from 1906-7; full of imagination, characteristic humor. Classic of great historical importance. Introduction by August Derleth. 32pp. 9¼ x 12¼. 23005-8 Pa. $2.00

LITTLE ORPHAN ANNIE AND LITTLE ORPHAN ANNIE IN COSMIC CITY, Harold Gray. Two great sequences from the early strips: our curly-haired heroine defends the Warbucks' financial empire and, then, takes on meanie Phineas P. Pinchpenny. Leapin' lizards! 178pp. 6⅛ x 8⅜. 23107-0 Pa. $2.00

ABSOLUTELY MAD INVENTIONS, A.E. Brown, H.A. Jeffcott. Hilarious, useless, or merely absurd inventions all granted patents by the U.S. Patent Office. Edible tie pin, mechanical hat tipper, etc. 57 illustrations. 125pp. 22596-8 Pa. $1.50

THE DEVIL'S DICTIONARY, Ambrose Bierce. Barbed, bitter, brilliant witticisms in the form of a dictionary. Best, most ferocious satire America has produced. 145pp. 20487-1 Pa. $1.75

CATALOGUE OF DOVER BOOKS

THE BEST DR. THORNDYKE DETECTIVE STORIES, R. Austin Freeman. The Case of Oscar Brodski, The Moabite Cipher, and 5 other favorites featuring the great scientific detective, plus his long-believed-lost first adventure — 31 New Inn — reprinted here for the first time. Edited by E.F. Bleiler. USO 20388-3 Pa. $3.00

BEST "THINKING MACHINE" DETECTIVE STORIES, Jacques Futrelle. The Problem of Cell 13 and 11 other stories about Prof. Augustus S.F.X. Van Dusen, including two "lost" stories. First reprinting of several. Edited by E.F. Bleiler. 241pp.
20537-1 Pa. $3.00

UNCLE SILAS, J. Sheridan LeFanu. Victorian Gothic mystery novel, considered by many best of period, even better than Collins or Dickens. Wonderful psychological terror. Introduction by Frederick Shroyer. 436pp. 21715-9 Pa. $4.50

BEST DR. POGGIOLI DETECTIVE STORIES, T.S. Stribling. 15 best stories from EQMM and The Saint offer new adventures in Mexico, Florida, Tennessee hills as Poggioli unravels mysteries and combats Count Jalacki. 217pp. 23227-1 Pa. $3.00

EIGHT DIME NOVELS, selected with an introduction by E.F. Bleiler. Adventures of Old King Brady, Frank James, Nick Carter, Deadwood Dick, Buffalo Bill, The Steam Man, Frank Merriwell, and Horatio Alger — 1877 to 1905. Important, entertaining popular literature in facsimile reprint, with original covers. 190pp. 9 x 12. 22975-0 Pa. $3.50

ALICE'S ADVENTURES UNDER GROUND, Lewis Carroll. Facsimile of ms. Carroll gave Alice Liddell in 1864. Different in many ways from final Alice. Handlettered, illustrated by Carroll. Introduction by Martin Gardner. 128pp. 21482-6 Pa. $2.00

ALICE IN WONDERLAND COLORING BOOK, Lewis Carroll. Pictures by John Tenniel. Large-size versions of the famous illustrations of Alice, Cheshire Cat, Mad Hatter and all the others, waiting for your crayons. Abridged text. 36 illustrations. 64pp. 8¼ x 11. 22853-3 Pa. $1.50

AVENTURES D'ALICE AU PAYS DES MERVEILLES, Lewis Carroll. Bué's translation of "Alice" into French, supervised by Carroll himself. Novel way to learn language. (No English text.) 42 Tenniel illustrations. 196pp. 22836-3 Pa. $3.00

MYTHS AND FOLK TALES OF IRELAND, Jeremiah Curtin. 11 stories that are Irish versions of European fairy tales and 9 stories from the Fenian cycle — 20 tales of legend and magic that comprise an essential work in the history of folklore. 256pp. 22430-9 Pa. $3.00

EAST O' THE SUN AND WEST O' THE MOON, George W. Dasent. Only full edition of favorite, wonderful Norwegian fairytales — Why the Sea is Salt, Boots and the Troll, etc. — with 77 illustrations by Kittelsen & Werenskiöld. 418pp.
22521-6 Pa. $4.50

PERRAULT'S FAIRY TALES, Charles Perrault and Gustave Doré. Original versions of Cinderella, Sleeping Beauty, Little Red Riding Hood, etc. in best translation, with 34 wonderful illustrations by Gustave Doré. 117pp. 8⅛ x 11. 22311-6 Pa. $2.50

EARLY NEW ENGLAND GRAVESTONE RUBBINGS, Edmund V. Gillon, Jr. 43 photographs, 226 rubbings show heavily symbolic, macabre, sometimes humorous primitive American art. Up to early 19th century. 207pp. 8⅜ x 11¼.
21380-3 Pa. $4.00

L.J.M. DAGUERRE: THE HISTORY OF THE DIORAMA AND THE DAGUERREOTYPE, Helmut and Alison Gernsheim. Definitive account. Early history, life and work of Daguerre; discovery of daguerreotype process; diffusion abroad; other early photography. 124 illustrations. 226pp. 6⅙ x 9¼.
22290-X Pa. $4.00

PHOTOGRAPHY AND THE AMERICAN SCENE, Robert Taft. The basic book on American photography as art, recording form, 1839-1889. Development, influence on society, great photographers, types (portraits, war, frontier, etc.), whatever else needed. Inexhaustible. Illustrated with 322 early photos, daguerreotypes, tintypes, stereo slides, etc. 546pp. 6⅛ x 9¼.
21201-7 Pa. $6.00

PHOTOGRAPHIC SKETCHBOOK OF THE CIVIL WAR, Alexander Gardner. Reproduction of 1866 volume with 100 on-the-field photographs: Manassas, Lincoln on battlefield, slave pens, etc. Introduction by E.F. Bleiler. 224pp. 10¾ x 9.
22731-6 Pa. $6.00

THE MOVIES: A PICTURE QUIZ BOOK, Stanley Appelbaum & Hayward Cirker. Match stars with their movies, name actors and actresses, test your movie skill with 241 stills from 236 great movies, 1902-1959. Indexes of performers and films. 128pp. 8⅜ x 9¼.
20222-4 Pa. $3.00

THE TALKIES, Richard Griffith. Anthology of features, articles from Photoplay, 1928-1940, reproduced complete. Stars, famous movies, technical features, fabulous ads, etc.; Garbo, Chaplin, King Kong, Lubitsch, etc. 4 color plates, scores of illustrations. 327pp. 8⅜ x 11¼.
22762-6 Pa. $6.95

THE MOVIE MUSICAL FROM VITAPHONE TO "42ND STREET," edited by Miles Kreuger. Relive the rise of the movie musical as reported in the pages of Photoplay magazine (1926-1933): every movie review, cast list, ad, and record review; every significant feature article, production still, biography, forecast, and gossip story. Profusely illustrated. 367pp. 8⅜ x 11¼.
23154-2 Pa. $7.95

JOHANN SEBASTIAN BACH, Philipp Spitta. Great classic of biography, musical commentary, with hundreds of pieces analyzed. Also good for Bach's contemporaries. 450 musical examples. Total of 1799pp.
EUK 22278-0, 22279-9 Clothbd., Two vol. set $25.00

BEETHOVEN AND HIS NINE SYMPHONIES, Sir George Grove. Thorough history, analysis, commentary on symphonies and some related pieces. For either beginner or advanced student. 436 musical passages. 407pp.
20334-4 Pa. $4.00

MOZART AND HIS PIANO CONCERTOS, Cuthbert Girdlestone. The only full-length study. Detailed analyses of all 21 concertos, sources; 417 musical examples. 509pp.
21271-8 Pa. $6.00

THE FITZWILLIAM VIRGINAL BOOK, edited by J. Fuller Maitland, W.B. Squire. Famous early 17th century collection of keyboard music, 300 works by Morley, Byrd, Bull, Gibbons, etc. Modern notation. Total of 938pp. 8⅜ x 11.
ECE 21068-5, 21069-3 Pa., Two vol. set $15.00

COMPLETE STRING QUARTETS, Wolfgang A. Mozart. Breitkopf and Härtel edition. All 23 string quartets plus alternate slow movement to K156. Study score. 277pp. 9⅜ x 12¼.
22372-8 Pa. $6.00

COMPLETE SONG CYCLES, Franz Schubert. Complete piano, vocal music of Die Schöne Müllerin, Die Winterreise, Schwanengesang. Also Drinker English singing translations. Breitkopf and Härtel edition. 217pp. 9⅜ x 12¼.
22649-2 Pa. $5.00

THE COMPLETE PRELUDES AND ETUDES FOR PIANOFORTE SOLO, Alexander Scriabin. All the preludes and etudes including many perfectly spun miniatures. Edited by K.N. Igumnov and Y.I. Mil'shteyn. 250pp. 9 x 12.
22919-X Pa. $6.00

TRISTAN UND ISOLDE, Richard Wagner. Full orchestral score with complete instrumentation. Do not confuse with piano reduction. Commentary by Felix Mottl, great Wagnerian conductor and scholar. Study score. 655pp. 8⅛ x 11.
22915-7 Pa. $11.95

FAVORITE SONGS OF THE NINETIES, ed. Robert Fremont. Full reproduction, including covers, of 88 favorites: Ta-Ra-Ra-Boom-De-Aye, The Band Played On, Bird in a Gilded Cage, Under the Bamboo Tree, After the Ball, etc. 401pp. 9 x 12.
EBE 21536-9 Pa. $6.95

SOUSA'S GREAT MARCHES IN PIANO TRANSCRIPTION: ORIGINAL SHEET MUSIC OF 23 WORKS, John Philip Sousa. Selected by Lester S. Levy. Playing edition includes: The Stars and Stripes Forever, The Thunderer, The Gladiator, King Cotton, Washington Post, much more. 24 illustrations. 111pp. 9 x 12.
USO 23132-1 Pa. $3.50

CLASSIC PIANO RAGS, selected with an introduction by Rudi Blesh. Best ragtime music (1897-1922) by Scott Joplin, James Scott, Joseph F. Lamb, Tom Turpin, 9 others. Printed from best original sheet music, plus covers. 364pp. 9 x 12.
EBE 20469-3 Pa. $7.50

ANALYSIS OF CHINESE CHARACTERS, C.D. Wilder, J.H. Ingram. 1000 most important characters analyzed according to primitives, phonetics, historical development. Traditional method offers mnemonic aid to beginner, intermediate student of Chinese, Japanese. 365pp.
23045-7 Pa. $4.00

MODERN CHINESE: A BASIC COURSE, Faculty of Peking University. Self study, classroom course in modern Mandarin. Records contain phonetics, vocabulary, sentences, lessons. 249 page book contains all recorded text, translations, grammar, vocabulary, exercises. Best course on market. 3 12" 33⅓ monaural records, book, album.
98832-5 Set $12.50

MANUAL OF THE TREES OF NORTH AMERICA, Charles S. Sargent. The basic survey of every native tree and tree-like shrub, 717 species in all. Extremely full descriptions, information on habitat, growth, locales, economics, etc. Necessary to every serious tree lover. Over 100 finding keys. 783 illustrations. Total of 986pp.
20277-1, 20278-X Pa., Two vol. set $9.00

BIRDS OF THE NEW YORK AREA, John Bull. Indispensable guide to more than 400 species within a hundred-mile radius of Manhattan. Information on range, status, breeding, migration, distribution trends, etc. Foreword by Roger Tory Peterson. 17 drawings; maps. 540pp.
23222-0 Pa. $6.00

THE SEA-BEACH AT EBB-TIDE, Augusta Foote Arnold. Identify hundreds of marine plants and animals: algae, seaweeds, squids, crabs, corals, etc. Descriptions cover food, life cycle, size, shape, habitat. Over 600 drawings. 490pp.
21949-6 Pa. $5.00

THE MOTH BOOK, William J. Holland. Identify more than 2,000 moths of North America. General information, precise species descriptions. 623 illustrations plus 48 color plates show almost all species, full size. 1968 edition. Still the basic book. Total of 551pp. 6½ x 9¼.
21948-8 Pa. $6.00

HOW INDIANS USE WILD PLANTS FOR FOOD, MEDICINE & CRAFTS, Frances Densmore. Smithsonian, Bureau of American Ethnology report presents wealth of material on nearly 200 plants used by Chippewas of Minnesota and Wisconsin. 33 plates plus 122pp. of text. 6⅛ x 9¼.
23019-8 Pa. $2.50

OLD NEW YORK IN EARLY PHOTOGRAPHS, edited by Mary Black. Your only chance to see New York City as it was 1853-1906, through 196 wonderful photographs from N.Y. Historical Society. Great Blizzard, Lincoln's funeral procession, great buildings. 228pp. 9 x 12.
22907-6 Pa. $6.95

THE AMERICAN REVOLUTION, A PICTURE SOURCEBOOK, John Grafton. Wonderful Bicentennial picture source, with 411 illustrations (contemporary and 19th century) showing battles, personalities, maps, events, flags, posters, soldier's life, ships, etc. all captioned and explained. A wonderful browsing book, supplement to other historical reading. 160pp. 9 x 12.
23226-3 Pa. $4.00

PERSONAL NARRATIVE OF A PILGRIMAGE TO AL-MADINAH AND MECCAH, Richard Burton. Great travel classic by remarkably colorful personality. Burton, disguised as a Moroccan, visited sacred shrines of Islam, narrowly escaping death. Wonderful observations of Islamic life, customs, personalities. 47 illustrations. Total of 959pp.
21217-3, 21218-1 Pa., Two vol. set $10.00

INCIDENTS OF TRAVEL IN CENTRAL AMERICA, CHIAPAS, AND YUCATAN, John L. Stephens. Almost single-handed discovery of Maya culture; exploration of ruined cities, monuments, temples; customs of Indians. 115 drawings. 892pp.
22404-X, 22405-8 Pa., Two vol. set $9.00

CONSTRUCTION OF AMERICAN FURNITURE TREASURES, Lester Margon. 344 detail drawings, complete text on constructing exact reproductions of 38 early American masterpieces: Hepplewhite sideboard, Duncan Phyfe drop-leaf table, mantel clock, gate-leg dining table, Pa. German cupboard, more. 38 plates. 54 photographs. 168pp. 8⅜ x 11¼.   23056-2 Pa. $4.00

JEWELRY MAKING AND DESIGN, Augustus F. Rose, Antonio Cirino. Professional secrets revealed in thorough, practical guide: tools, materials, processes; rings, brooches, chains, cast pieces, enamelling, setting stones, etc. Do not confuse with skimpy introductions: beginner can use, professional can learn from it. Over 200 illustrations. 306pp.   21750-7 Pa. $3.00

METALWORK AND ENAMELLING, Herbert Maryon. Generally conceded best all-around book. Countless trade secrets: materials, tools, soldering, filigree, setting, inlay, niello, repoussé, casting, polishing, etc. For beginner or expert. Author was foremost British expert. 330 illustrations. 335pp.   22702-2 Pa. $4.00

WEAVING WITH FOOT-POWER LOOMS, Edward F. Worst. Setting up a loom, beginning to weave, constructing equipment, using dyes, more, plus over 285 drafts of traditional patterns including Colonial and Swedish weaves. More than 200 other figures. For beginning and advanced. 275pp. 8¾ x 6⅜ .   23064-3 Pa. $4.50

WEAVING A NAVAJO BLANKET, Gladys A. Reichard. Foremost anthropologist studied under Navajo women, reveals every step in process from wool, dyeing, spinning, setting up loom, designing, weaving. Much history, symbolism. With this book you could make one yourself. 97 illustrations. 222pp.   22992-0 Pa. $3.00

NATURAL DYES AND HOME DYEING, Rita J. Adrosko. Use natural ingredients: bark, flowers, leaves, lichens, insects etc. Over 135 specific recipes from historical sources for cotton, wool, other fabrics. Genuine premodern handicrafts. 12 illustrations. 160pp.   22688-3 Pa. $2.00

DRIED FLOWERS, Sarah Whitlock and Martha Rankin. Concise, clear, practical guide to dehydration, glycerinizing, pressing plant material, and more. Covers use of silica gel. 12 drawings. Originally titled "New Techniques with Dried Flowers." 32pp.   21802-3 Pa. $1.00

THOMAS NAST: CARTOONS AND ILLUSTRATIONS, with text by Thomas Nast St. Hill. Father of American political cartooning. Cartoons that destroyed Tweed Ring; inflation, free love, church and state; original Republican elephant and Democratic donkey; Santa Claus; more. 117 illustrations. 146pp. 9 x 12.
22983-1 Pa. $4.00
23067-8 Clothbd. $8.50

FREDERIC REMINGTON: 173 DRAWINGS AND ILLUSTRATIONS. Most famous of the Western artists, most responsible for our myths about the American West in its untamed days. Complete reprinting of *Drawings of Frederic Remington* (1897), plus other selections. 4 additional drawings in color on covers. 140pp. 9 x 12.
20714-5 Pa. **$5.00**

CATALOGUE OF DOVER BOOKS

How to Solve Chess Problems, Kenneth S. Howard. Practical suggestions on problem solving for very beginners. 58 two-move problems, 46 3-movers, 8 4-movers for practice, plus hints. 171pp. 20748-X Pa. $3.00

A Guide to Fairy Chess, Anthony Dickins. 3-D chess, 4-D chess, chess on a cylindrical board, reflecting pieces that bounce off edges, cooperative chess, retrograde chess, maximummers, much more. Most based on work of great Dawson. Full handbook, 100 problems. 66pp. 7⅞ x 10¾. 22687-5 Pa. $2.00

Win at Backgammon, Millard Hopper. Best opening moves, running game, blocking game, back game, tables of odds, etc. Hopper makes the game clear enough for anyone to play, and win. 43 diagrams. 111pp. 22894-0 Pa. $1.50

Bidding a Bridge Hand, Terence Reese. Master player "thinks out loud" the binding of 75 hands that defy point count systems. Organized by bidding problem—no-fit situations, overbidding, underbidding, cueing your defense, etc. 254pp. EBE 22830-4 Pa. $3.00

The Precision Bidding System in Bridge, C.C. Wei, edited by Alan Truscott. Inventor of precision bidding presents average hands and hands from actual play, including games from 1969 Bermuda Bowl where system emerged. 114 exercises. 116pp. 21171-1 Pa. $2.25

Learn Magic, Henry Hay. 20 simple, easy-to-follow lessons on magic for the new magician: illusions, card tricks, silks, sleights of hand, coin manipulations, escapes, and more —all with a minimum amount of equipment. Final chapter explains the great stage illusions. 92 illustrations. 285pp. 21238-6 Pa. $2.95

The New Magician's Manual, Walter B. Gibson. Step-by-step instructions and clear illustrations guide the novice in mastering 36 tricks; much equipment supplied on 16 pages of cut-out materials. 36 additional tricks. 64 illustrations. 159pp. 6⅝ x 10. 23113-5 Pa. $3.00

Professional Magic for Amateurs, Walter B. Gibson. 50 easy, effective tricks used by professionals —cards, string, tumblers, handkerchiefs, mental magic, etc. 63 illustrations. 223pp. 23012-0 Pa. $2.50

Card Manipulations, Jean Hugard. Very rich collection of manipulations; has taught thousands of fine magicians tricks that are really workable, eye-catching. Easily followed, serious work. Over 200 illustrations. 163pp. 20539-8 Pa. $2.00

Abbott's Encyclopedia of Rope Tricks for Magicians, Stewart James. Complete reference book for amateur and professional magicians containing more than 150 tricks involving knots, penetrations, cut and restored rope, etc. 510 illustrations. Reprint of 3rd edition. 400pp. 23206-9 Pa. $3.50

The Secrets of Houdini, J.C. Cannell. Classic study of Houdini's incredible magic, exposing closely-kept professional secrets and revealing, in general terms, the whole art of stage magic. 67 illustrations. 279pp. 22913-0 Pa. $3.00

CATALOGUE OF DOVER BOOKS

THE MAGIC MOVING PICTURE BOOK, Bliss, Sands & Co. The pictures in this book move! Volcanoes erupt, a house burns, a serpentine dancer wiggles her way through a number. By using a specially ruled acetate screen provided, you can obtain these and 15 other startling effects. Originally "The Motograph Moving Picture Book." 32pp. 8¼ x 11. 23224-7 Pa. $1.75

STRING FIGURES AND HOW TO MAKE THEM, Caroline F. Jayne. Fullest, clearest instructions on string figures from around world: Eskimo, Navajo, Lapp, Europe, more. Cats cradle, moving spear, lightning, stars. Introduction by A.C. Haddon. 950 illustrations. 407pp. 20152-X Pa. $3.50

PAPER FOLDING FOR BEGINNERS, William D. Murray and Francis J. Rigney. Clearest book on market for making origami sail boats, roosters, frogs that move legs, cups, bonbon boxes. 40 projects. More than 275 illustrations. Photographs. 94pp. 20713-7 Pa $1.50

INDIAN SIGN LANGUAGE, William Tomkins. Over 525 signs developed by Sioux, Blackfoot, Cheyenne, Arapahoe and other tribes. Written instructions and diagrams: how to make words, construct sentences. Also 290 pictographs of Sioux and Ojibway tribes. 111pp. 6⅛ x 9¼. 22029-X Pa. $1.75

BOOMERANGS: HOW TO MAKE AND THROW THEM, Bernard S. Mason. Easy to make and throw, dozens of designs: cross-stick, pinwheel, boomabird, tumblestick, Australian curved stick boomerang. Complete throwing instructions. All safe. 99pp. 23028-7 Pa. $1.75

25 KITES THAT FLY, Leslie Hunt. Full, easy to follow instructions for kites made from inexpensive materials. Many novelties. Reeling, raising, designing your own. 70 illustrations. 110pp. 22550-X Pa. $1.50

TRICKS AND GAMES ON THE POOL TABLE, Fred Herrmann. 79 tricks and games, some solitaires, some for 2 or more players, some competitive; mystifying shots and throws, unusual carom, tricks involving cork, coins, a hat, more. 77 figures. 95pp. 21814-7 Pa. $1.50

WOODCRAFT AND CAMPING, Bernard S. Mason. How to make a quick emergency shelter, select woods that will burn immediately, make do with limited supplies, etc. Also making many things out of wood, rawhide, bark, at camp. Formerly titled Woodcraft. 295 illustrations. 580pp. 21951-8 Pa. $4.00

AN INTRODUCTION TO CHESS MOVES AND TACTICS SIMPLY EXPLAINED, Leonard Barden. Informal intermediate introduction: reasons for moves, tactics, openings, traps, positional play, endgame. Isolates patterns. 102pp. USO 21210-6 Pa. $1.35

LASKER'S MANUAL OF CHESS, Dr. Emanuel Lasker. Great world champion offers very thorough coverage of all aspects of chess. Combinations, position play, openings, endgame, aesthetics of chess, philosophy of struggle, much more. Filled with analyzed games. 390pp. 20640-8 Pa. $4.00

SLEEPING BEAUTY, illustrated by Arthur Rackham. Perhaps the fullest, most delightful version ever, told by C.S. Evans. Rackham's best work. 49 illustrations. 110pp. 7⅞ x 10¾.
22756-1 Pa. $2.00

THE WONDERFUL WIZARD OF OZ, L. Frank Baum. Facsimile in full color of America's finest children's classic. Introduction by Martin Gardner. 143 illustrations by W.W. Denslow. 267pp.
20691-2 Pa. $3.50

GOOPS AND HOW TO BE THEM, Gelett Burgess. Classic tongue-in-cheek masquerading as etiquette book. 87 verses, 170 cartoons as Goops demonstrate virtues of table manners, neatness, courtesy, more. 88pp. 6½ x 9¼.
22233-0 Pa. $2.00

THE BROWNIES, THEIR BOOK, Palmer Cox. Small as mice, cunning as foxes, exuberant, mischievous, Brownies go to zoo, toy shop, seashore, circus, more. 24 verse adventures. 266 illustrations. 144pp. 6⅝ x 9¼.
21265-3 Pa. $2.50

BILLY WHISKERS: THE AUTOBIOGRAPHY OF A GOAT, Frances Trego Montgomery. Escapades of that rambunctious goat. Favorite from turn of the century America. 24 illustrations. 259pp.
22345-0 Pa. $2.75

THE ROCKET BOOK, Peter Newell. Fritz, janitor's kid, sets off rocket in basement of apartment house; an ingenious hole punched through every page traces course of rocket. 22 duotone drawings, verses. 48pp. 6⅞ x 8⅜.
22044-3 Pa. $1.50

CUT AND COLOR PAPER MASKS, Michael Grater. Clowns, animals, funny faces . . . simply color them in, cut them out, and put them together, and you have 9 paper masks to play with and enjoy. Complete instructions. Assembled masks shown in full color on the covers. 32pp. 8¼ x 11.
23171-2 Pa. $1.50

THE TALE OF PETER RABBIT, Beatrix Potter. The inimitable Peter's terrifying adventure in Mr. McGregor's garden, with all 27 wonderful, full-color Potter illustrations. 55pp. 4¼ x 5½.
USO 22827-4 Pa. $1.00

THE TALE OF MRS. TIGGY-WINKLE, Beatrix Potter. Your child will love this story about a very special hedgehog and all 27 wonderful, full-color Potter illustrations. 57pp. 4¼ x 5½.
USO 20546-0 Pa. $1.00

THE TALE OF BENJAMIN BUNNY, Beatrix Potter. Peter Rabbit's cousin coaxes him back into Mr. McGregor's garden for a whole new set of adventures. A favorite with children. All 27 full-color illustrations. 59pp. 4¼ x 5½.
USO 21102-9 Pa. $1.00

THE MERRY ADVENTURES OF ROBIN HOOD, Howard Pyle. Facsimile of original (1883) edition, finest modern version of English outlaw's adventures. 23 illustrations by Pyle. 296pp. 6½ x 9¼.
22043-5 Pa. $4.00

TWO LITTLE SAVAGES, Ernest Thompson Seton. Adventures of two boys who lived as Indians; explaining Indian ways, woodlore, pioneer methods. 293 illustrations. 286pp.
20985-7 Pa. $3.50

HOUDINI ON MAGIC, Harold Houdini. Edited by Walter Gibson, Morris N. Young. How he escaped; exposés of fake spiritualists; instructions for eye-catching tricks; other fascinating material by and about greatest magician. 155 illustrations. 280pp.
20384-0 Pa. $2.75

HANDBOOK OF THE NUTRITIONAL CONTENTS OF FOOD, U.S. Dept. of Agriculture. Largest, most detailed source of food nutrition information ever prepared. Two mammoth tables: one measuring nutrients in 100 grams of edible portion; the other, in edible portion of 1 pound as purchased. Originally titled Composition of Foods. 190pp. 9 x 12.
21342-0 Pa. $4.00

COMPLETE GUIDE TO HOME CANNING, PRESERVING AND FREEZING, U.S. Dept. of Agriculture. Seven basic manuals with full instructions for jams and jellies; pickles and relishes; canning fruits, vegetables, meat; freezing anything. Really good recipes, exact instructions for optimal results. Save a fortune in food. 156 illustrations. 214pp. 6⅛ x 9¼.
22911-4 Pa. $2.50

THE BREAD TRAY, Louis P. De Gouy. Nearly every bread the cook could buy or make: bread sticks of Italy, fruit breads of Greece, glazed rolls of Vienna, everything from corn pone to croissants. Over 500 recipes altogether. including buns, rolls, muffins, scones, and more. 463pp.
23000-7 Pa. $4.00

CREATIVE HAMBURGER COOKERY, Louis P. De Gouy. 182 unusual recipes for casseroles, meat loaves and hamburgers that turn inexpensive ground meat into memorable main dishes: Arizona chili burgers, burger tamale pie, burger stew, burger corn loaf, burger wine loaf, and more. 120pp.
23001-5 Pa. $1.75

LONG ISLAND SEAFOOD COOKBOOK, J. George Frederick and Jean Joyce. Probably the best American seafood cookbook. Hundreds of recipes. 40 gourmet sauces, 123 recipes using oysters alone! All varieties of fish and seafood amply represented. 324pp.
22677-8 Pa. $3.50

THE EPICUREAN: A COMPLETE TREATISE OF ANALYTICAL AND PRACTICAL STUDIES IN THE CULINARY ART, Charles Ranhofer. Great modern classic. 3,500 recipes from master chef of Delmonico's, turn-of-the-century America's best restaurant. Also explained, many techniques known only to professional chefs. 775 illustrations. 1183pp. 6⅝ x 10.
22680-8 Clothbd. $22.50

THE AMERICAN WINE COOK BOOK, Ted Hatch. Over 700 recipes: old favorites livened up with wine plus many more: Czech fish soup, quince soup, sauce Perigueux, shrimp shortcake, filets Stroganoff, cordon bleu goulash, jambonneau, wine fruit cake, more. 314pp.
22796-0 Pa. $2.50

DELICIOUS VEGETARIAN COOKING, Ivan Baker. Close to 500 delicious and varied recipes: soups, main course dishes (pea, bean, lentil, cheese, vegetable, pasta, and egg dishes), savories, stews, whole-wheat breads and cakes, more. 168pp.
USO 22834-7 Pa. $2.00

COOKIES FROM MANY LANDS, Josephine Perry. Crullers, oatmeal cookies, chaux au chocolate, English tea cakes, mandel kuchen, Sacher torte, Danish puff pastry, Swedish cookies — a mouth-watering collection of 223 recipes. 157pp.

22832-0 Pa. $2.25

ROSE RECIPES, Eleanour S. Rohde. How to make sauces, jellies, tarts, salads, pot-pourris, sweet bags, pomanders, perfumes from garden roses; all exact recipes. Century old favorites. 95pp.

22957-2 Pa. $1.75

"OSCAR" OF THE WALDORF'S COOKBOOK, Oscar Tschirky. Famous American chef reveals 3455 recipes that made Waldorf great; cream of French, German, American cooking, in all categories. Full instructions, easy home use. 1896 edition. 907pp. 6⅝ x 9⅜.

20790-0 Clothbd. $15.00

JAMS AND JELLIES, May Byron. Over 500 old-time recipes for delicious jams, jellies, marmalades, preserves, and many other items. Probably the largest jam and jelly book in print. Originally titled May Byron's Jam Book. 276pp.

USO 23130-5 Pa. $3.50

MUSHROOM RECIPES, André L. Simon. 110 recipes for everyday and special cooking. Champignons à la grecque, sole bonne femme, chicken liver croustades, more; 9 basic sauces, 13 ways of cooking mushrooms. 54pp.

USO 20913-X Pa. $1.25

THE BUCKEYE COOKBOOK, Buckeye Publishing Company. Over 1,000 easy-to-follow, traditional recipes from the American Midwest: bread (100 recipes alone), meat, game, jam, candy, cake, ice cream, and many other categories of cooking. 64 illustrations. From 1883 enlarged edition. 416pp.

23218-2 Pa. $4.00

TWENTY-TWO AUTHENTIC BANQUETS FROM INDIA, Robert H. Christie. Complete, easy-to-do recipes for almost 200 authentic Indian dishes assembled in 22 banquets. Arranged by region. Selected from Banquets of the Nations. 192pp.

23200-X Pa. $2.50